Lost

IN WEST TEXAS

Lost

IN WEST TEXAS

ILLUSTRATED BY THE AUTHOR

Jim W. Corder

Texas A&M University Press

COLLEGE STATION

Library of Congress Cataloging-in-Publication Data

Corder, Jim W. (Jim Wayne,) 1929–
  Lost in west Texas.

  (A Wardlaw book)
  I. Texas—Social life and customs. I. Title.
II. Series.
F391.C765 1988   976.4   87-10217
ISBN 0-89096-363-0 (alk. paper)

For David, Becky, Jenny,
Cathy, Mindy, Bin,
and Andrew

Contents

Lost
IN WEST TEXAS

How I Got Lost

The first time I had to fill out a form that inquired about the place of my birth, it took me the better part of a day to get the job done. I'm pretty easily intimidated, of course. Fourth-grade teachers and shoe salesmen intimidate me; so do ministers and bus drivers and my mother. If I have to speak to a boss, I go up to him or her practicing my first sentence. Forms intimidate me a little bit, too, and make me apprehensive. There're always so many things that one *might* say in reply to the questions on a form. And there's the other problem. My mother taught me to try to be polite, and I always try to say what I think they want on the forms. Well, anyway, it all started when I had to fill out some kind of form in high school, I think it was.

One section asked for the place of my birth. Now, as I understand the matter, I was born in a farmhouse several miles outside Jayton, Texas, but I didn't think I had room to put all of that down, and it didn't seem like they would want all of that, anyway. So I put down Jayton as the place of my birth. Then I waited for several weeks thinking about what I should have done and expecting to be called to the principal's office and made to put it right, if I were lucky enough to get off with that. But nothing happened.

Then sometime later, I was drafted, and there was another form to fill out. But this time it was the United States Army, and I thought that Jayton just wouldn't do. I thought for sure that at least one official somewhere would know from his statistics and records that Jayton is in one county and the farmhouse where I was born is in the neighboring county. I couldn't put down Jay-

ton, but I couldn't put down any town in the other county either because you don't mess around with the United States Army. So I finally just put down Stonewall County, where the little house was. That bothered me for a good while. For one thing, it seemed presumptuous to claim a whole county for the place of my birth.

Nothing happened, but the sorry business doesn't end there. While I was in the Army, I got married. Now a thing that has the sanction of church and state is a thing to be careful with, and there was another form to be filled out before we could get the marriage license. I reckoned I had been flirting all along with criminal charges for fraudulent answers, so this time I put all my faith in authority and announced that the place of my birth was Aspermont, Texas. At the time, I had never been *in* Aspermont; I had been *through* Aspermont. But since that is the county seat of the county in which the little farmhouse was located, I thought somehow that I must be recorded there. And besides that, there used to be a real nice statue of Justice in front of the old courthouse there.

Well, the rest is brief to tell. In time we had a son, who in time was given a birth certificate, and they wanted to know where I was born. This time in sheer bravado and in my pride at being a father, I threw caution to the winds and wrote down that the place of my birth was Spur, Texas. I never lived in Spur, but it seemed like more people on the outside would have heard of it. Spur had a rodeo once, and a swimming pool made of concrete, and was once headquarters for a big ranch. It was a kind of status symbol, you see, and I had sold out.

4

That's how it all came about. That's how I got lost. Later, I discovered that my wife had been going around filling out forms and telling about the place of my birth. She isn't as familiar with that part of Texas as I am, and all those years she put down places for me like Spur, and Stamford, and Lubbock, and Odessa, and Turkey, and Quitaque, and Matador. What I had done, she helped with, as she vowed to. As far as I know, no one on earth knows for sure where I was born. My parents could say, but we don't talk about it much anymore.

Late Word from the Provinces

If you could go from Fort Worth straight as the crow flies just a little to the north of west, you'd be there after about 180 miles, though I don't know, actually, that I've ever seen a crow fly straight. The way there by the wavering, bending route that people take is longer by a little, maybe 195 miles. The road, though a little crooked, is chiefly west, as most of the roads I take are. I've been by and glanced at those easterly and southerly stretches of Texas, but find myself feeling choked and edgy there, the air too low and heavy, the trees too near and copious. The road I've mentioned goes into the lonesome middle of country that just barely begins along a line that lies generally north and south down from the Red River through Fort Worth and on to Austin before it angles off southwestward toward the Rio Grande. Texas has been split along that axis before: Anglo-Americans moved across the territory as far as that Fort Worth–Austin line as early as the 1830s, and they were still stalled there in the 1860s because they knew that out beyond that line the lonesome country was chancy and the Comanches were lords. The census of 1870 shows that only thirty-three towns and cities in the state were able to report a population, and all thirty-three were east of the line down across the state through Fort Worth and Austin.

But I was saying that if you go from Fort Worth—better, I expect, by the crooked road than by the crow's path—just a little north of west you'll be there after about 180, or maybe 195 miles. You'll understand that I don't mean the main western road that

goes through Abilene to Big Spring and on to El Paso, nor yet do I mean the other major road that goes through Wichita Falls and into the Panhandle and Amarillo. I mean a quieter road in between.

This road takes you from Fort Worth through Weatherford and on to Mineral Wells. Out of Mineral Wells it runs down through the rough Brazos country and across the Brazos, and then you're in the long, mostly straight, and generally uncluttered stretch to Breckenridge. I remember riding that road, much rougher then, in 1941 with my aunt—she was young then, and frisky, though she's not now. It was an early summer night, and the moon was big, and its light was bright and clean and lovely, and she decided that the world was so clear with moonlight she could drive without the headlights, and she did, and we drove for miles enthralled. Albany is next. Just at the near edge of Albany a farm road splits off to the north that will take you to the ruins of Fort Griffin, a staging ground for the last campaigns against the Comanches, and the jumping-off place for the hunters who slaughtered the last of the buffalo in the late 1870s. On the yonder side of Albany the road splits and the northwesterly branch takes you to Leuders—I don't know much about Leuders but do remember a loud bawdy song that the older boys once brought back from a church camp there—and on to Stamford. Out of Stamford the road goes past Sagerton to Aspermont.

When you get to Aspermont, you're there. "There" is just around a long curve on the other side of town. "There," off to the left in the blue distance, blue above the broken plain surrounding them—the Double Mountains.

If you're acquainted with mountains, the Double Mountains would look to you like two hills. They rise to an elevation of maybe seventeen hundred feet, always blue—I never saw them otherwise—on the horizon of my youth, always present, the markers of that province.

I have come this long way to the Double Mountains for a particular reason. God lives on top of the Double Mountains.

This may be startling news to some of my theologically disposed colleagues, who are still searching for God, whether on high, or out there, or in here, and to some of my philosophically disposed colleagues, who haven't yet commenced the search, wanting first to complete their inquiries into his-slash-her nature. Startling though it may be, it is nevertheless true. God abides on top of the Double Mountains.

And that's not all. The Double Mountains are not only the dwelling place of God, but also, as the markers of my province, they are the first boundary of the cosmos.

The cosmos, as I am able to apprehend it, stretches from the Double Mountains northwestward some forty miles to the Big Rock Candy Mountain. On up that road from Aspermont, through Swenson, through Jayton, where my family lived, past Girard, I'd see it after a while off to the left. But you wouldn't see it. It's not there any more.

The Big Rock Candy Mountain was an outcropping more than a hill, I guess, and mostly rock. My father worked for the State Highway Department in 1937 while they made gravel for the new highway out of the mountain. We moved for the short term to a two-room house not far away. From the edge of the mesquite-strewn pasture that was our backyard, I could see the mountain and see the chunks chewed out of it as they ground the world to gravel. I remember my father coming home, his eyes red from the dust, his body still jumping and jerking from the jackhammer. He made two dollars a day.

One day we looked, and the machines had eaten all of the Big Rock Candy Mountain. It was gone when we looked. I would see it if I drove that way, but I can't tell you how to find it. You wouldn't see it.

But it is the other end of the cosmos. Cosmos stretched from the Double Mountains to that gone hill. In between lay Swenson and Jayton (where my family returned) and Girard and Spur. Most importantly, in between lay the Croton Breaks, my own wondrous middle earth. In these years since, I have left this cosmos. I have ignored it. I have, I do believe, lived awhile elsewhere. But it is still my province, my cosmos, still there just over the horizon. I can almost see it when I sit on the front porch.

A year or so ago an elderly lady wearing a red tam spent several weeks evangelizing among students and others on the campus where I teach. Almost every morning she would take her place on the sidewalk that runs along the east side of University Drive. She would stand sort of between the old Science Building and the library so that she was in a main line of student traffic between classes. When I first encountered her, I didn't know it, but her opening to all she stopped was, "Where do you expect to go when you die?"

I had been to the library and was headed back, angling out of the way a little, thinking I'd go by the post office before I went back to the office. That's how I fell to meet her—it came from angling out of the way a little.

"Where do you expect to go when you die?" she asked me.

Now I'm not too good with answers even when I've practiced, and hers wasn't the kind of question that you get too many chances to practice on in an ordinary day. I didn't know what to say. To claim that I had a ticket for heaven seemed unrealistic. But then to declare that hell's my destination seemed a vain and prideful thing to do. So I told her that if it was all the same to her and to all concerned, I believed that I'd just go to the Croton Breaks.

I suppose that most folks would just as soon not make that trip. And there may be some who'd say that going to Croton Breaks is going to hell. I can see their way of thinking—one's no improvement over the other so far as annual rainfall is concerned. But anyway, that's what I told her.

The Croton Breaks make the middle of the cosmos I have sketched. You won't find them marked on some maps, but all maps will show a great empty space, a rough square using up parts of four counties, marked at four vague corners by Aspermont on the southeast, Jayton on the southwest, Spur on the northwest, and Guthrie on the northeast, where the Four Sixes Ranch falls into the bad country. Mr. J. W. Williams, in his book *The Big Ranch Country*, offers first prize to the Croton Breaks for bad country in Texas and tells of a roundup on the Matador

8

Ranch in 1936 when cowmen finally flushed out of the Breaks some old cows wearing a brand that hadn't been used in seventeen years.

No towns lie in the Breaks. They stretch thirty to forty miles most any direction. Winding through the south is the Salt Fork of the Brazos River, and winding through all over is Croton Creek, mostly dry. An old reconnaissance soil survey says the soil is Vernon very fine sandy loam, consisting of six to ten inches of a brown to chocolate-brown very fine sandy loam underlain by chocolate-brown loam or very fine sandy loam passing at about two feet into a reddish-yellow loam that carries considerable grayish calcareous material.

The Breaks are an eroded plain, a network of shallow gullies, deep gullies, deep mysterious canyons, dry stream courses with steep, sometimes vertical walls. They have their name from Col. Randolph Marcy, who crossed the area in 1849, tending goldrushers on their way west, marking out spots for cavalry forts on his return trip. He thought the waters of the creek he came to, of high mineral content and highly antithetical to constipation, were reminiscent of similarly curative waters from Croton Springs in New York. So it came to be Croton Creek, and the area came to be the Croton Breaks.

But when I lived in Jayton, along their southwest edge, as I did until I was twelve or so, I didn't even know the name. I knew the stretch of country only as "the canyons." The first falling-off place was about ten yards from our back door, and I knew my corner of the canyons in a way not told by reconnaissance soil surveys, from days and hours alone, poking here and there, naming a dry waterfall in one place, marking the way to a special "lost canyon" in another, marveling at a dry watercourse just the width, at its bottom, of my foot from some rivulet an eon ago. It was the center of my cosmology, then, when I thought the top of a windmill was high, and the Double Mountains near Aspermont were the southerly end of earth, and the Big Rock Candy Mountain was the other end of everything.

So when I said that I would just as soon go to the Croton Breaks, I intended no flippancy to the lady in the red tam. I meant her no disrespect. For quiet, I couldn't find a better place, and maybe, for knowing: the earth opens itself up in layers there, and each

9

rock that falls after an age's pushing from the side of a gully reveals another surprise. But only if you go slow, and are willing to wait and watch, hunkered.

This is my province, though I think I have at least squatter's rights in others. Its outer dimensions, you may conclude, are narrow, but I will reply that its middle is wide and varied. This is my province. I am a provincial.

And I'm undisturbed about being provincial. Each of us lives in a province, though not all are measured in the same way. Some are spatial. Some are temporal. Some are familial. Some are urban. Some are rural. Some are walled by bigotry and ignorance. Size has little to do with province. Some people can make a province of a hemisphere or out of a skin color. Each of us lives in a province, and we measure the world's dimensions by our own.

A province is a prison only if you do not know that it is a province. If you wait and watch and listen, you'll know that any province abuts and overlaps and entwines with all others. I keep trying to learn how the Double Mountains are sisters to the mountains that rise beyond South Fork in Colorado, how the waters lapping at the pier in Rotterdam once lapped at the sides of the Double Mountains. I keep trying to learn how tomorrow's cosmos is visible in today's. I know the past is still there; though an age has vanished, the Big Rock Candy Mountain still stands plain against the sky off to the left of the road that runs northwestward through my cosmos.

Episodes in the Life of a West Texas Materialist

My family moved to Fort Worth late in the fall of 1939 so that my father could take a job at Purina Mill, though it held no promise of regularity. He had looked for work already in Abilene and Lubbock and Sweetwater, and there was none. He came to the city alone, and looked for days before he heard that they were hiring at the mill. "They offered me thirty-two cents an hour," he remarked during the small ceremony at his retirement in 1970, "and I called Momma and told her to *Send My Tools.*" My mother and brother and I joined him about three weeks later.

I remember riding the lonely stretch through the shinnery below the Double Mountains from Jayton to Aspermont, but then I must have slept, for after that I remember only rousing at the concern I heard in the voices—we would learn later that what they had suspected was trouble was only the roar cars commonly made on the brick highway between Mineral Wells and Weatherford—and again, struck by some sleepy whim to think that the big blue neon FRIGIDAIRE over the building across from Montgomery Ward was frozen there.

In the next nine months or so I finished the fourth grade, and we moved four times. Then, late in the summer of 1940, they took my father on permanently at the mill.

I wasn't there to see it, but my brother was, and he told me about how my father learned the news that they wanted him permanently. I had heard it, too, from Mr. Needham, our neighbor, who told the story to me more than once in the years to come. In one of the layoffs from the mill, my father had found a short-term job with a threshing crew working just north of the city—in fields now covered with a large school, a scattered warren of apartments, and a helicopter plant—and then, a few days later, found that the crew could use my brother as well, though he was only fifteen. I remember little about the summer: the city had opened a branch library in the school I went to just a few blocks away, and I discovered books; but I do remember my brother falling asleep in the bathtub, early evenings, after he'd come in from work with my father.

Mr. Needham, our neighbor, already had a regular job, and my father had given Purina Mill Mr. Needham's telephone number just in case they decided they needed him. "We were working way down at the end of the field farthest from the road," my brother told me later, "and I looked up, way down the field, and saw Mr. Needham's car coming along the road, and I figured the telephone call had come, and so I started running. And then I was going real good, the first thing I know I looked up and here came Poppa barreling past me." There's nothing much either notable or funny about that, except when you are ten, as I was, or fifteen, as my brother was, and think that your father is an old man. That way, running is pretty funny, and outrunning a fifteen-year-old is really funny. Then Mr. Needham would take up the story: "I looked down the way and saw ole Nolan raising a cloud of dust. 'Bout half way down the row he reached up and got his hat in his hand, and here he came, just flogging it."

We had lived until then in Jayton. Jayton lies twenty-five miles or so south of the main highway from Fort Worth through Seymour to Lubbock, and some thirty-five miles below the Caprock and the Staked Plains. If you stood on the school grounds and looked south, you could see the Double Mountains, blue no matter the weather; if you looked west, you couldn't see much of anything except the cemetery and more country; if you looked north, it was about the same; if you looked northeast and east and didn't watch where you were going, you'd fall into the Croton Breaks. I spent a lot of time there, and expected that they went on—ravines and washes twining and twining, red dirt and white rocks—probably forever and finally learned much later that they did run on past the northeast corner of the county, along much of Stonewall County to the east and much of Dickens and King counties to the north.

The population of Jayton was 750 when we lived there. Annual rainfall had dropped and dropped again, from about thirty inches in 1933 to about twenty-one inches in each of the decade's later years, and those inches came mostly at the wrong times, so I wasn't too surprised some years later when Mr. Walter Prescott Webb said that we'd been living on the edge of the Great American Desert. And the dust had come, days on end. I never could stay long in the room where my wife was ironing; something in the heat and smell set red dirt swirling in my head.

As the dust blew before the wind and blew again, and as the rainfall dropped and dropped again, cotton production fell. My father worked at the oil mill in Jayton, and his work, as well as that of all the hands, lasted only as long as the cotton crop. I remember a certain jubilation one year when the mill stayed open for nine months, and he worked twelve hours a day, seven days a week. Most years it was less, therefore my father came to be hunting work in Lubbock and Abilene and Sweetwater and finally Fort Worth. While we lived in Jayton, and while the mill was closed, he worked wherever he could. During one spring and summer he worked for the State Highway Department, breaking rocks with a jackhammer for two dollars a day. We'd moved north of Jayton toward Spur into an old two-room house on the back end of a farm that wasn't much good on the front end either, and I could see across several miles to the rise and hill where he worked. I was pretty sure it was the Big Rock Candy Mountain, but they kept biting chunks out of it, and it grew smaller.

But even if the Big Rock Candy Mountain diminished before my eyes, I didn't know we were poor. When the mill fired up again, we moved back to Jayton in time for school. I was with my friends, and had the Croton Breaks in my backyard, and I didn't know we were poor. Still, there were times.

Times, I'd say, when the presence of poverty had crept into my bones and I knew it without knowing it, times I recall even now only with a cold scary feel that shudders up my back until my shoulders shake to discard the moment and rid me of the recollection.

13

I remember a Christmas. It was, I believe, the same Christmas that we had the huge tree. On a Sunday afternoon my mother and father and brother and I went out into the Breaks, hunting a cedar to be our Christmas tree. We hunted a long while, my mother doubting tree after tree, before we found a great tall almost-straight tree. "Tree was so big," my father would say years later, "I had to cut it off three times before I could get it in the house." "Well," my mother would say, "I knew there wasn't going to be much under it, so I thought we could at least have a big tree." I believe it was that same Christmas.

My brother and I each got a ball glove—nothing else, and no matter, that was God's own plenty, in that year of Joe DiMaggio. They'd come earlier in that year's package from Sears Roebuck, though of course my brother and I didn't know that, thinking the package that came in September had only that year's shirts and overalls for school.

On Christmas morning there they were. Mine was darker and had Red Rolfe's name on it; his was lighter, yellowish, and was graced with Charley Gehringer.

Now a ball glove is a particular consideration. I do not know what tokens of other generations than mine compare with a ball glove, what holds talismanic power for other boys. To me, a ball glove was a conclusion, a beatific resolution: there was no place else to be, nothing else to aspire to. I had played softball before school and after school and at lunchtime and in the summer, hours on hours, and I had, alone, batted rocks into the canyon with the handle of a pickax. And now there was a ball glove, and it was still there the next morning.

Tokens and talismans, too, are forgotten, hence the fall of totems to rot among weeds, and the decay of churches. In the course of time, I treated the ball glove as small boys sometimes treat things. I forgot it, and left it lying overnight on the porch. The next morning it was in the front yard. The small dog that lived with us had chewed on it some and scuffed it around, teething and playing.

As it happened, I was able later to stuff and sew and salvage my glove; it was with me when we moved to Fort Worth, and for some years after. But I guess it wasn't a talisman any more. In the moments when I stood and looked at it lying there torn in the yard, and in the longer moments when I sat or walked down in the canyon, carrying it with me, I knew that there wouldn't be another glove, not that year, perhaps not the next. Indeed, so far as I could tell then, there would never be another glove. I couldn't have said it, I know, could only feel a tightening of the self, but when I left the glove out and lost its special mark, its patina of grace, I lost, too, a moment of achieved style.

My crises, though grinding at the time of their rise and fall, are typically minor. I remember, too, a certain nickel that didn't stay lost.

The Texas Theater was a sometime thing, its operation risked first by this, then by that itinerant magnate. There was no way for a boy to become habituated to its pleasures, money seldom being available simultaneously with its operation, and so the sense of Saturday afternoon at the Texas was particularly keen.

I remember a Saturday morning when my brother and I courted our mother, dancing our attendances upon her with glad chores and other uncharacteristic behaviors. She gave us the four nickels we needed at last, after prolonging her reluctance so that she might savor our performances, and we left for the Texas, each with two nickels in hand, though my brother, being older and more sophisticated, simply dropped his in his pocket. Our path took us across a corner of a field, across the highway, thence down the road that would become the west boundary of the square. Somehow, stooping through the fence on the far side of the field, I dropped one nickel.

In time, on our hands and knees in the red dust, we found it, but the moments between the loss and the finding have never ended for me. There were no more nickels at home. One didn't even ask to determine whether there were more. I knew that. My brother knew that. He stood and stooped and looked and stood again, divided many ways by his anger with me, his intense wish to be at the Texas, his impatience with such a situation and such a little brother, and his great care for me.

And I remember my father's railroad watch, during the years since my memory began in Jayton and in the years after we moved to the city, though I didn't find out the truth about it until just the other day. My mother keeps it on the dresser now, for he seldom carries it, and between them they once in a while remember to wind it. Sometimes back then when we were all young, it would slow and stop, and he would shake it and say, "We're all out of time. I guess it's gone." Then he would listen and wind, or put it away, and when I would ask to see or hold it, it would be gone to the jeweler's shop. "Mostly," he'd say, "you couldn't own a better watch, but now the time's all gone."

A heavy railroad watch, it was a dusty sun swinging from a square-linked golden chain, and it ticked pew-quiet to crying babies, patience to skittish boys. On Sundays, when I surrendered my overalls for pants and so had belt loops, he would hook the bar on the chain there; then I would be otherwise than six, or eight, and the watch, a chancy handful, would hoist me older by my own watch pocket. And I would feel time and rub my fingers golden, and fret its feel.

I think I have the feeling still in my fingers when the children pester me now at my desk to see the arrowhead all over again. It has the patina, too, of good hard things shaped and shaded by the rivers of time and trouble. It is a good point, well made, perhaps two inches long, and I tell myself likely Comanche. But I do not know that it is Comanche—it may be that a Kiowa thumb tested it—or who chipped it by what fire. I remember the feel of the watch from the days in Jayton, and from the edgy days in the city.

We were visiting my parents, and I was sipping the sweet tea that's best at the bottom of the last glass if you can keep the ice from cascading down your front, and with one thing and another I fell to complaining about yard work. "Used to," I remember saying, "we just swept the yard once in a while." My mother for once was talkative, and so we sat over the spoils of dinner, and I rearranged a full belly to suit my lap and chair while we told hard times. They would watch the sky go brass and purple and dark with Dakota come to Texas. She remembered the job my father took when the mill closed, grinding rocks on a mountain to make gravel for a road. He came home fevered many a day, she remembered, body still jerking from the hammer, and just two dollars for the day. Sometimes then, when we were still buying water for the cistern by the dirty barrel-load, or later when we first moved to the city, the money would go, and there would be nothing.

Those were the times, she told me as if I had always known, when he would go and pawn the watch.

And finally, I remember erasing all that was written on sheets of tablet paper—after the homework was checked and my fourth-grade teacher had returned it—so that I could use the paper again. My parents didn't tell me to do this; so far as I know they didn't know that I did it, and so far as I know to this moment it was not necessary for me to do this. I don't think I thought of myself then, nor do I now, as a fourth-grade martyr, marvelous if minor, but I guess by then I had decided that we were poor.

"What do you make of this?" Boswell would sometimes inquire, when he had in a letter related to his friend some quirky, contradictory, impulsive episodes of his recent days. "What do you make of this?"

These are leftovers. What do I make of them? Perhaps only a poor and watery stew of a cautionary tale.

My generation and my father's have been accused of materialism, crass, cold, and unthinking. I expect the charge is true, and false, as most charges are, but I owe a word or two on my father's account, if not my own.

If we were and are materialistic, as charged, we weren't and aren't too successful. He still yearns after a cabin in the country that he'll never have. He ran up the rows of that field to the job at the mill and stayed there thirty years, but I've already had all the inheritance there'll be from him. I know that there are acres of asses—men of his generation and mine—in suburbs and salesrooms and corporations, men who trivialized themselves for gain, but if he and I trivialized ourselves, it wasn't for gain.

But perhaps we weren't materialists after all. I reckon we are as messy and real and contradictory as men in most generations. That ball glove wasn't an object; it was a style, a hope, a capacity. When my father came running up the row, fast at first, then reaching up and grabbing his hat in his hand so that he could really go, he wasn't running after money. The choiceless life of poverty is abrasive, destructive, vinegary to the soul. We wanted to choose, he and I, to put on other modes of life, to hear other songs.

At the Mill:
Scenes from the Thirties

I

The troubleshooter down at the mill didn't want any pissant dollar and nickel man telling him what to do. Or how. He made a dollar fifteen. That was per day, you understand.

2

For a while there, we had enough dust blow in to make a new county every year. We didn't always used to be this high above sea level, you know.

3

If it rained some, we'd have a little cotton. If we had a little cotton, the gin would start up. If the gin did business, the oil mill would run.

We'd fire up along in September, early October. First thing, you know, we had to gin the seeds all over again, to get that little bitty fuzz off—we called it "linters."

The linters got baled up just like cotton and sold for padding and cheap mattresses, but mostly it went to munitions plants to make gunpowder and packing.

Then we'd hull the seeds, roll them, and put them in the big old cookers, and then they'd go, all cooked and soft, into the row of presses, and the hydraulics would squeeze the hot oil right out of them.

The caked seeds got broken up and sold for cow feed. The oil went off somewhere to turn into Crisco. Linters, seed, and oil—I tell you, we used those seeds plumb up.

And let me tell you, you take a cold baked sweet potato or a biscuit and dip it in that hot oil on a raw noon, and you'd get well and fat real quick.

4

When there was rain just right, and the cotton would hold out and come in, the mill might run seven, maybe eight months. Other times, we shut her down in three.

Then the mill boss would loan us the truck—you know, had the big bed and the slat sides—and we'd pile in that thing and go forty miles to Rotan. Rotan was a fair-size place then. That's where we went, everybody in that big old truck, to sign up for unemployment pay.

Then there'd be days and weeks and months of domino games, in the back of the drugstore, on the porch at the grocery, in the shade alongside the filling station, days and weeks of hunkering and figuring, days and weeks of grown men shooting marbles down by the mill. By and by somebody would get up, stretch from the morning's work and say, "Time for the noon whistle, boys, Mama'll have dinner on the table."

How Indians Got the Dance

When the cucumbers were pickles, dilled in Mason jars, and the ground was hot and hard, I pulled the played-out spring plants, clearing against the fall.

On August 8, I broke the ground again and left the skin of my right hand on the handle of the spading fork.

On August 9, I covered that with compost, mulched myself, filled my shoes, and got so dirty I was required to leave my pants on the back porch.

On August 10, I turned the compost under, soaked it down, and hoped for rest, good rain, and early supper.

And then the time had come. On the following day I broke and plowed and raked and drew two furrows. Then I turned to the Ferry-Morse cucumber scripture, Cucumber—Hybrid Table-treat, two months to table size, ten calories per portion. I put the seeds four inches apart and laid an inch of soil above. The text required that soil be tamped with care around the seeds. I stood at the furrow's end, then side-step danced down the row to bed the seeds, and hummed my song. The Indians found their dance in this, I told my daughter, made a dance from a hum and a side-step shuffle to bed the seed, binding them to earth. She laughed and said I was probably crazy and said she'd not believe me, but I think she did.

Outhouses, Belly Buttons, Weather Changes, Driving in West Texas, and Aunts, Dear Aunts

I

I didn't expect to be an antique so soon, but it seems to have worked out that way. The geographical and social circumstances of my early years are such that I find myself remembering things that few of my contemporaries and none of my juniors seem to recall. Clearly, then, I must be at least a generation older than I thought, contemporary with my elders.

Together with my elders—and our number grows fewer each year, threatening the loss from our culture of certain artifacts known only to our dwindling memory—together, I was saying, with my elders, I remember the outhouse.

The outhouses I have known best were structures ordinarily of wood, about five feet square, or less, standing some six feet high in front, the roof slanting downward to a rear wall of maybe four and one-half feet. The two sides were sometimes decorated with designs cut into the wood, the crescent moon and the diamond being the most widely favored figures. In some instances, the door was so decorated rather than the walls, and in a few instances, both the sides and the door were adorned, though the discriminating thought that made entirely too busy an effect. The outhouses of my memory were almost all of the gray-brown

21

achieved by weathering on unpainted wood. Some few, to be sure, were painted, but it seemed an affectation, and I recall that if, on a Halloween night, the choice presented itself to a group of boys between a painted and weathered outhouse, there was no contest as to which got toppled over.

When I was young and all of the family gathered on a holiday —Christmas, say—at my grandparents' farm, the outhouse there was the centerpiece for a regular entertainment. It was the custom of the gathered cousins—I don't know how many there were, and I believe that on two different occasions strangers joined the gathering undetected—to spend a portion of one morning chunking rocks at the outhouse. When it was empty, this was practice; when it was occupied, this was fun. It was a game that required both skill in the throwing arm and keen judgment, for some of the adults, when they went to the outhouse, wouldn't do as targets. Aunt Edith, for example, and Aunt Willie Mae were both entirely too gentle and ladylike, too quietly refined, for us to intrude upon their world. Any uncle would do. But Aunt Nell was out of bounds for particular and practical reasons: she was too young and frisky; she would chunk rocks back at us when she came out, she had a good arm and a sure aim, and she could whip most of us at wrestling. Aunt Cora, though, was just right. If we threw rocks at the outhouse while she was in it, she could be counted on to roar and bellow at us from inside, and then to emerge with the proper bluster and simulated rage. And she never could throw straight.

My experiences of outhouses are otherwise pretty ordinary, and I am not at all moved to lament their passing. Given, on the one hand, their quaint association in the minds of some with our past, their signal contribution to the imagined picturesqueness of a vanishing landscape, and given, on the other hand, the virulence of our occasional nostalgia crazes, I shall not be surprised to see offered one day soon in the annual Neiman-Marcus Christmas catalog a darling outhouse, adaptable for use as a bar and intended as a focal point of a lovely designed scene in the back part of the estate grounds.

If it's all the same to everyone concerned, I believe I'll not buy one. The outhouses of my recollection were unbearable in the summer's heat, shocking in the winter's cold, and terrifying in the night's darkness. Once in a while, they provided a moment's amusement for the assembled cousins, and that moment makes a fond memory. Otherwise, they're best put into the past.

Best put into the past, too, are cars that had to be cranked and lamps that made scant light for reading and chancy ovens and untreated, often fatal smallpox. All are best put into the past and left there. I think I understand our sometime zeal for the past, our sometime nostalgia for a gone world. The past is dear and deep in us, inescapably in our sinews. Aunt Nell is still young and frisky in my mind, and I hold her there. I know that we can be in the past, warmed and accompanied by the past. I know that the past should not imprison us, but free us, but oh, I wish I could find it, know it, see what it looked like when I wasn't watching, get testimony, know Aunt Edith's story, and Aunt Willie Mae's, and Aunt Cora's, and Aunt Nell's, and all the rest.

2

I'm usually a little doubtful when I hear someone who is caught up in reminiscence begin a sentence with "We'd always. . . ." Not much of anything is always. The cousins didn't chunk rocks at the outhouse during *every* family holiday gathering, usually only at Christmas, Thanksgiving, and July 4. I seem to remember spending a good part of each July 4 sitting on a folded quilt on top of an ice cream freezer, to hold it down while some uncle turned the crank. We did chunk rocks often enough for it to seem a regular entertainment. We're likely, we humans, to take an event that occurred sometimes and elevate it to a standard ritual, just as we're likely to take ourselves and our memory as the measure by which we know things.

Most speakers and writers use their own history and their own preferences as the standards by which to judge everything else. As for myself, for example, I have all creation arranged. Its center runs up my chest. Chicago is always *up* there, Atlanta is always *over* there, Houston is always *down* there, and Santa Fe is always *out* there. The prepositions take their direction from me, and my belly button is clearly the center of the cosmos. Most of us are when we speak. Consequently, when we look around us and see the world on the way to ruin or wherever and young people going around being different from us, we're likely to say, "Well, things weren't like this when *I* was young," or "What in the world are they teaching in school these days?" or "We knew how to study in my day," or "We had to toe the mark in our day—not like these kids today, don't have to do anything if they don't want to." Memory, even faulty memory, becomes actuality, and the way things seemed to be when we thought we were looking at them becomes in our mind the ways things really were.

I had, for example, always taken for granted that the circumstances and atmosphere of my upbringing were "normal" and that whatever deviated from this ambience was "abnormal." And yet I learned the other day that my environment was not normal at all. Professor Reid Bryson, a climatologist from the University of Wisconsin, says that the period from 1930 to 1960, roughly the first thirty years of my life, "was the most abnormal period in a thousand years—abnormally mild."

I can't, you see, quite be sure that I have understood what I have seen, and I don't know what things were like at all when I wasn't watching. But oh, I wish I could find it all, know it, get testimony.

3

But I do have images of Aunt Nell that I will keep uncorrected in my mind. I don't remember the year—it was early in World War II, and I was maybe thirteen. My family had moved from West Texas to Fort Worth, and we didn't go back because gas was rationed and our tires were thin and our car was old. For some reason, Aunt Nell came to Fort Worth—I was mostly oblivious of most things. Since it was summer and school was out, my parents said I could drive back to West Texas with Aunt Nell and stay with my grandparents at the farm. The moon was full and big beyond imagining. The moonlight was bright and clean and lovely, and the world was clear, and there were no cars but ours on the road. In the long stretch between Mineral Wells and Breckenridge, Aunt Nell decided that the moonlight was so bright she believed she could just about drive without the headlights on, and so she did. I thought it was exciting and brave and beautiful, and rode for miles in the clear world, enthralled. I am still enthralled.

4

That was a long time ago. Now it is February, 1986. Aunt Nell died on December 10, 1985. She was a long time dying. We had planned that I would drive my parents to Levelland, where Aunt Nell lived, for the funeral. But when the time came, an ice storm had moved across the state, the roads were sheeted and slick, and we were not able to get to where she was. I never did get to where she was, I guess, never learned her story, wasn't sure what she was like when I was watching, never knew what she was like when I wasn't looking, but I remember riding with her in the bright moonlight.

The Friday Game, or the Near-Athlete in West Texas

Not long ago, on a Friday evening in early October just after dark, I took a flight from Memphis back home to Fort Worth. Along the way, I saw lovely jewels below me and didn't realize until I had seen a couple what it was that I was seeing. It was, remember, a Friday evening. We were passing over town after town. Those pretty baubles below, green ovals set in bright gold, were football fields, and the Friday game was being played by high-school teams from Memphis to Fort Worth and on beyond. Seeing them called back old times, other Fridays, though there were no lights at the field in Jayton in 1938, and no planes flew overhead.

As I was growing up—and in my mind, that was still going on this morning—I was an ardent, though inadequately motivated and insufficiently directed, jock, clear through to my bone marrow. I'd like to explain a little why this is so, and why so little came of it.

When I first went to school, my family lived in a town that claimed some 750 souls in population—that doesn't include Boone

25

Bilberry, who, according to the Baptists, didn't have a soul. I went to school in that little town through the fourth grade. My brother was five years older than I. When he was in the ninth grade, the year before we moved to the city, Jayton High School decided that it could field a football team for the first time in history. If you are demographically agile, you'll soon reckon that a town of 750 souls—not counting Boone Bilberry—wouldn't have a large number of high-school-age males. At any rate, my brother played on the varsity team while he was in the ninth grade and again in the tenth grade until we moved to the city. It's what one did if one was a young male with any sense. I went and watched practice most days, and on one of the early days saw the principal drawing the yard lines off with a hoe. Once, when he reached the side near where I was standing, he turned, squinted along the line he had drawn in the dirt, turned back to me, and said, "Well, it'd look straight to a blind man." That's the only time I ever talked to the principal.

At any rate, though baseball was my true first love, football was what a young male did in a small West Texas town. I expected to be a football player. I had some natural though untutored ability, and probably would have been a football player in that small town. But we moved to the city, and there were more folks, and some of them were a whole lot larger. By the time I was a junior in high school, I had my full height, six feet, but I weighed only 135 pounds and somewhere I had acquired an entirely unjustified regard for the well-being of my ungainly person, and so I abandoned football. Thereafter, I was mostly a runner, though I played baseball and softball. I played on an Army team that was good enough to be thrashed thoroughly by another Army team that won the European theater championship. Then I played on a church softball team until the behavior of my knees, the instructions of my doctor, and the suggestions of my teammates caused me to retire at age forty-five. I'm still disappointed that I didn't turn out to be Joe DiMaggio.

I've lingered over my sports career, which existed mostly in my mind, in order to try to indicate that I am not inherently and fundamentally opposed to athletics. I have to linger a while longer over the earlier years because of important things that happened in the same year. It was 1938, and we still lived in the little town of 750 souls, less Boone Bilberry.

Rilke remarks somewhere, "Don't think life is more than what's packed into childhood." What got packed into 1938 was particularly important to me. I discovered universities. I'm not sure that I knew colleges and universities existed before that time. I probably did, but they had made no great impression on me. But in 1938 my family got a radio, and quite by accident I discovered that football games were broadcast on Saturday afternoons. Listening to any one game taught me the names of universities all across the land because of the broadcasters' habit of periodically announcing scores from other games. I heard for the first time the music of university bands at halftime. But most of all I discovered Davey O'Brien, Ki Aldrich, Connie Sparks, Don Looney, I. B. Hale, and all the others on TCU's 1938 national championship team. They came to personify both football and the idea of a university. This last, as it turned out, was I suppose one of the two or three most significant ideas of my life. I heard about them all that fall.

First they beat Centenary, and the headline on September 24 read, "O'Brien's Long Shots Down Gents, 13–10." Then they beat Arkansas, and the headline said, "Frogs' Power Outlasts Porker Passes, 21–14." Then they played Temple University, and the headline said, "Frogs Smash Owls in Second Period, 28–6." Next was A&M and the headline said, "Frogs Smash Aggies, 34–6! Aldrich, O'Brien Star." Then it was Marquette: "Frogs Strike Quickly, Coast to 21–0 Victory." Baylor was next: "Frogs Smash Bears with Power, Passes, 39–7." Then came a simple headline "Frogs Beat Tulsa, 21–0." The headline on Sunday, November 12, said "O'Brien's Passes Sink Texas, 28–6." Then they played Rice, and the headline read, "Frogs' Passes Punish Owls, 29–7." Finally, the headline for Sunday, November 26, said, "Frogs Use Power to Beat Ponies, 20–7, for Conference Title."

Well, if you're about nine, expecting and wanting to be a football player, and have just discovered a university only some 250 miles away, it just doesn't get any better than that.

Then at Christmas I got the first book I ever owned all by myself, *Andy at Yale*, and it told about Andy and his new acquain-

tances at Yale and how the lads went out for football. Just a little
later, TCU played Carnegie Tech in the Sugar Bowl and won, 15–7.

It was quite a year: I learned about universities, which have
been at the center of my life ever since, and I learned about them
in the most thrilling way—through the romanticized accounts
of *Andy at Yale,* and through the deeds of Davey O'Brien and the
1938 national championship team at TCU in Fort Worth, and I
knew folks who had actually been in Fort Worth. It wasn't on
another planet. That old feeling doesn't go away easily: "Don't
think life is more than what's packed into childhood." It still
comes sometimes when I see the grace of a defensive back going
high into a crowd and taking away the pass they don't want him
to have, or when I see a clean block that breaks a running back
loose, or especially when I see a quarterback throw a forty-yard
pass that drops right over the left shoulder and into the hands
of an end who's going full out down the sideline.

That old feeling doesn't go away easily, and I suppose it never
goes away entirely, but it fades because one learns other lessons,
fades, fades, until there's nothing left but a whisper of old time.

I still watch football games on television sometimes, and pout
if the team I favor happens to lose. In 1938 I thought I was hearing and reading about athletes who not only personified the university, but who were also known and cared for by their class-
mates. I've learned, though, that *Andy at Yale* described a world
that may never have existed, or if it did, it has long since disappeared. One doesn't simply "go out" for football much these
days, and most athletes are known to the student body at large
only as stereotypes. And besides, that world of *Andy at Yale* was
all-white and elitist.

Nothing much turned out the way I imagined it would. I guess
I'm a little shocked, but not much surprised. A couple of years
ago Jayton changed over to six-man football, and in the fall, 1985,
won the state championship. I'm glad for the players and for the
school and town, but it isn't quite the same in my mind as that
glorious game when I saw my brother go high in the air to inter-
cept that pass.

Most things aren't quite the same. Those jewels in towns across
the country are bright only once in a while, and football is not
what I had somehow wanted it to be. Neither am I, for that mat-

ter. I didn't become Sammy Baugh or Davey O'Brien or Tommy Harmon or John Kimbrough—or Joe DiMaggio.

Against a Mournful Wind

In the spring of 1980, a citizen would have to be wonderfully innocent, unaware of television, unfamiliar with newspapers, uncommonly insensitive, and in general about three bricks shy of a load not to suspect that the future is perilous for all of us, for education and educators in particular. I'm inclined to think, as I've heard it said, that if on some days at least we're not fretful, worried, and a little psychotic as we contemplate the future, that probably means that we can't have a very good grasp on reality.

When I was young, alone, say, in the house with my family gone, and trees or something mysterious scratched against the roof and a settling in the house made steps creak, or alone, say, walking home in the dark after seeing *The Mummy Walks*, I thought that if I would go ahead and name the ghosts that were out there, it would somehow be better and I could breathe again. I expect I still feel that way. If we acknowledge and name the anxieties, fears, difficulties, and problems that are out there waiting for us, they don't go away, to be sure, but they're not quite so scary. It's easier to deal with the ghost behind the next tree if you have a name for it.

We look ahead and wonder if there is a future for education. The future of education is always at stake, probably, but we don't always know it. We know it now. Our conception of ourselves as teachers is at stake, too, and our vision of education is in doubt. Out there (in the future we are sometimes unwilling to look at) the possibility of liberal education seems in doubt. If we don't look and see what's there, we can't go except with stumbling, halting steps, and partly blind.

But of course we can't see all that is out there. The future isn't here yet. We see signs and portents, but not all are revealed to us, and we don't understand some that are. We can't be perfect in wisdom, but we can learn to face the frights, perils, and signs of despair that we see.

29

Sometimes, everything seems to be coming loose. Part of what startles us and sometimes very nearly renders us inactive is that the myths, assumptions, professional dicta, and good advice we started with all appear, on some days, to be little more than an accumulation of rubbish, a pile of things that were obsolete long before they were discarded. Somehow or another, we were all taught that thrift is important, but through most of our lives no one has acted as if it were. We were taught, in one way or another, of the need for human community, but we move, disband, and dissociate. In one way or another, we were taught, or we thought we were, the rewards of love, marriage, and fidelity, and everyone knows what has happened to those things. We were taught that the world is spacious and full of promise, but it shrank and our expectations shrank with it. In one way or another, we were taught the proper content for our disciplines, but they have changed six or twenty times, shifting out from under us. Disciplines come and disciplines go, and subjects we held dear are prized no longer. Sometimes, everything seems to be coming loose.

I don't want to linger indefinitely over the possibilities of disaster, but I do want to display for a moment a quick catalog of failures, perils, and fears. My list of impending woes is not complete, nor is it the same as another would compile, but it will do for now.

This morning's paper detailed on the first page, and for column after column inside, the effects of proposed federal budget cuts. Naturally enough, education is one of the first places likely to experience further budget reductions. Elsewhere in this morning's paper, a visiting expert teaches us that "less is more," that it really feels better to have less. If that is so, then we'll get the chance to feel just fine.

But we don't have to look outside educational establishments for problems. Inside, we have often acted as if our work were sacred. We have often acted as if things must continue to be what they have been, as if our disciplines must remain inviolate as we first conceived them, when in fact we have in many instances long since lost any sense of rigorous definition or clarification of our hopes and expectations for the humanities, the social sciences, and the natural sciences. It's already apparent that traditional programs will not survive in the next generation or so, at least not in their present form. But we seldom look at the signs, therefore don't know what's happening, therefore can't anticipate what to do next. The number of history students and English students has dropped dramatically across the country; many schools are down to about 30 percent of the enrollments they had in these fields in their peak years. Language study has in some places gone very nearly into the negative numbers. The response, sometimes, has been to scurry into haphazard experiments or to deny change and cling to curricula of the past.

But other problems wait inside the academy. We forget that education should be first of all concerned with the free spirit of free citizens. We forget that all of us are first men and women, and in our schools move instead to train students as if they were first lawyers, management entrepreneurs, doctors, English scholars, chemists, accountants.

If the prospect for education seems gloomy and chancy, in other words, we are ourselves partly responsible. We are not prepared to provide or willing to provide what the world may ask for. We create false divisions among ourselves, and we can't talk across the boundaries of our disciplines and departments. We divide ourselves into parts, and then each part or discipline or department cherishes itself as the only or at least the best of truth. Our own language betrays us, and we splinter into a new Babel of conflicting groups, each with its own strange tongue. We succumb to a new parochialism: only about 3 percent of all undergraduate students in the country are enrolled in any studies dealing with international affairs or foreign peoples and cultures. And on the rare occasions when we gather to talk about planning for the future, we talk about tight money, retrenchment, FTE's and faculty/student ratios, and credit-hour production. We get lost in instrumentalities and seldom talk about an imagined future that is both proper and exciting for our work.

If we look, the problems increase and multiply, both without and within. We haven't yet taught our students to be men and women of understanding and learning; they and we are still creatures of ambition, greed, and war. We haven't yet learned ourselves or taught others how to face crucial shortages in energy and food, pollution of water and land, tense overcrowding in some

pockets, barrenness and empty poverty in others. Political confusion and economic uncertainty have shaken the people's faith
in education as a key to the future. Education has been the pre-
sumed path to upward mobility. Now both are under question.
Educational institutions have come under serious doubt; some
people tell us, "You are not doing your job very well"; and others
say, "We really don't need what you have to offer." Some already
think that upward mobility is impossible. If education is not wor-
thy and upward mobility is not possible, then we may face a
stratified, class-bound society ruled by a self-perpetuating power
elite. Signals have already flared: the back-to-the-basics movement
that has swirled around us—and it will not soon go away—
promises, if we are not vigilant, to turn into a profound reaction-
ary movement that is social and political before it is educational.

If we look, we can indeed see failures, perils, and fears. Robert
Lekachman ended an essay on the future of education in a re-
cent issue of *Change* in this way: "As a good American should,
I should like to end on a note of cheer. My misfortune is that
I can't identify a single valid reason to be cheerful about the out-
look for education."

To be sure, another would explain our problems in a different
way. One thing seems certain, however: we can't be what we are
and become what we should be.

If what I have said seems too dismal, too full of woe, too
narrowly pessimistic, perhaps there is a small remedy. Looking
a different way does often let us discover something different
to see.

I want to tell about a house—more accurately, a small ruin.
The walls still stand, and part of a rotting roof, from which pro-
trudes part of a rusty stovepipe. Even if I offered explicit directions, many would not find it. You'd have to go west from Fort
Worth, Texas, about 225 miles, through Weatherford, Mineral
Wells, Breckenridge, Albany, Stamford, Aspermont, Swenson, to
Jayton. By now, you'd be into territory from which it costs about
fourteen dollars to send a letter to the world, but you'd still not
be there yet. Jayton, with a population of about 750, is the last
big city before you get there. You drive four or five miles out of
Jayton, turn onto a dirt road, and drive deep into what people
in the area call the Croton Breaks for seven or eight miles, and

after a while you'd come to the little community known as Golden Pond. It's not close to anything. Nobody ever goes there. It's no longer recognizable as a community. The only inhabitants are ghosts, and the southwest wind keens and moans through rotting planks of an occasional ruined shack.

Not far from Golden Pond—some two miles or so—is the house I mentioned. It's a little house made of native stone. It measures about ten feet by twelve feet, and there is a small wooden lean-to on the back. You can see through the walls. It's empty, obviously has been for years.

My family and I happened onto this house a few years ago. We stopped to photograph it—to city folks, it looked picturesque. Not long afterward, I chanced to show the photograph to one of my aunts. She shuddered, quite noticeably, and said she didn't want to see it, or to think about it.

As it turned out, she lived in that house with a family during the school year of 1933–34 while she taught at Golden Pond School. It was her first teaching job, and she made twelve dollars a month with room and board thrown in. She remarked, incidentally, that you could see through the walls in 1933, too, and feel the wind coming through.

For a moment, it's worth remembering that house, that school, my aunt, and that school year, 1933–34. It's worth trying to think what it was like, that first teaching job at twelve dollars a month, living in that house in that place.

She was far miles from home. There were no telephones in

Golden Pond, and she had no transportation save what her feet offered. Even in 1933 there were no cars in Golden Pond. She was there among strangers in a barren, twisty land. That area, the Croton Breaks, is broken, eroded country; dry creeks, ravines, gullies, and canyons break the terrain for thirty miles and more. Even in 1933 it was rough country, nearly forgotten country.

There were no telephones, no electricity, no running water, no way to wash except in a pan or a round metal washtub. And the wind whistled and moaned between the rocks.

If you stand on the little rise between ravines where the rock house is, if you stand there even in bright daylight, in every direction you look the distance is blue and far and melancholy. It is the lonesomest country I know. If you stand there at night, imagine what the dark is like when you're far from home and there's only one dingy, smoky kerosene lamp, which for the sake of economy, can't be burned long.

Imagine lying in a narrow bed with the wind coming in between the rocks and across you, or moaning over and through the inadequate roof.

Imagine that, if you will, and then inquire: Lying there in the lonesome dark, with the wind keening and moaning over you, how could you possibly imagine a bright future?

I've told about this house in that place so that I could come to this: at any given moment, the future can always look grim. Indeed, since going into the future means becoming something other than what we are now—that is, it's always risky—then the future is always grim until someone makes it otherwise. A future always happens; a good future has to be made.

Future making is teachers' work. The myth of Sisyphus, Camus taught us, tells much about human work and human futures. Everything depends upon how we feel about the rock and the work of pushing it. If sadness and defeat clench us and melancholy rises in our hearts, then the rock wins. But if we know that we always have the chance to keep making a future, that next time we'll get the rock up the top of the hill, then we and the future win. If we know this, it's because we learned it from a good teacher, wherever he or she happens to be located, whatever he or she happens to be called at the moment. It's always a good teacher who makes the future for us. Some teachers, of course, just reiterate the past. Some grab the prevailing fashions of the present. But good teachers make the future.

Because we are mostly pretty complex, we are easily lost to each other. Sometimes our vanity teaches us that other people are only what we perceive them to be, and we lose each other by our ignorance, our unwillingness to search each other out and know each other. Sometimes we are apart, sometimes forlorn, sometimes afraid. We are segmented, divided into parts; we focus narrowly sometimes so that we can see more intently. But a good teacher can unite us in the imaginative consideration of learning. We are isolated from each other and often compartmentalized, but a good teacher can teach us to touch hands with others, to learn from others, to take the encouragement we need from others, to remember that there is no sure sign of wisdom that marks a single department, discipline, or college. A good teacher can teach us that it is splendid to be human together.

A good teacher can teach us to know that each of us is blessed with a startling gift: each can be his or her own advocate, judge, critic, spokesman. A good teacher can teach us that change did not cease when it reached us, that we can go into a new world clasping to our memories what was dear in the old, but expecting to make magic hereafter. A good teacher can teach us that it is all right to question orthodoxy, that everything is full of wonder if we watch, that creation is too rich and varied and copious to be comprehended by single visions. There are many ways of looking, and a good teacher can show us many visions, each holding something precious and dear. Dear and deep as the past may be to us, a good teacher will teach us that we are free to remain unimpressed with what we have been and to be intent instead upon what we are becoming. Good teachers have the surest, boldest, loveliest validation for their work. Teaching by its nature takes hold of the past in order to proclaim and to create the future. However dark the time may be, good teachers are always making the future.

When they refuse to lock themselves into some pattern of the past, when they refuse to acquiesce in prevailing fashions, when they teach the nation's citizens the ultimate practical and spiritual uses of education, the liberating uses of knowledge, when their own behavior is self-luminous, then good teachers will teach

LOST IN WEST TEXAS

us to make a future brighter than any we can now imagine. And then the rest of us will not be alone and frightened by a mournful, moaning wind in a small rock house in a dark and lonesome country.

Everything Used to Be a Weed

In years past I have taken some modest pleasure in mowing the lawn. The ritualistic nature of the process offers some simple comforts. In the green season there is a teeming, squirming life among the blades, the grass seems to grow behind the mower, and the copiousness of life twined secretly in the grass seems to promise birth and rebirth. Always before I felt I could lace my fingers in the thick mat of the lawn and feel the tremors and stirrings of growth in my hands and up along my arms.

It is a little harder to do now. The lawn mower has grown heavier. The yard is wider than it was, and its slopes are higher. Weights real or imagined sometimes encumber my hands and arms. Woes real or imagined sometimes interrupt the current of hope I thought I felt rising through the grass. Sometimes, just as I sag behind the mower, the world seems to sag as well, and I think I am not alone in these sorry circumstances.

Sometimes we all sag. Sometimes our energy slackens, and there comes crowding in on us a host of alarms, perils, and fears. At times we suffer, as Norman Cousins has put it, from a sense of helplessness that derives from a collective perception of imminent defeat, from the imperfection of human organization, from onrushing depersonalization, from the dread of loneliness (*Saturday Review*, December 4, 1973). Robert Heilbroner frightens us with his assurance in *An Inquiry into the Human Prospect*: "The answer to whether we can conceive of the future other than as a continuation of the darkness, cruelty, and disorder of the past seems to me to be no; and to the question of whether worse impends, yes." Norman Borlaug, called the "father of the green revolution" for his development of high-yield cereal grains, predicted in June, 1974, the early possibility of famine and an attendant epidemic of 10 to 50 million deaths.

The National Center for Atmospheric Research announced in November, 1975, that a catastrophic drought is overdue for the U.S. Great Plains. Any news medium on any day will add accounts of war, poverty, and violations both of the flesh and of the spirit. A single section of a single issue of almost any local newspaper is likely to raise our anxiety with accounts of assassination plots, of our impending desperation for energy resources, of army training for biological warfare, of war in the Middle East, of the Social Security system's going in the red, of the success of pornographic films, and of the possibility that both coffee and bacon may be cancer-inducing.

Susan Sontag, writing in the *New York Times* of February 8, 1976, says, "This civilization, already so far overtaken by barbarism, is at an end, and nothing we do will put it back together again." We are advised by *Saturday Review* that "the traditional program of liberal arts in undergraduate education has crumbled" (July 22, 1974) and that "America is in headlong retreat from its commitment to education" (March 20, 1976). Teachers doubt what they're to hand down to the next generation and wonder if anyone will take it if it's handed. Disciplines of learning that we have cherished seem in peril of extinction. Job markets shift, and while good people called to vocation are abandoned, others thrive who seem to have no vocation except to manipulate their fellow beings. We are already almost entombed in mounds of paper, files, forms, and printouts, and we are always being deluded, not by grandeur, but by triviality. If we can't find ailments enough outside, we can bore ourselves to death. Meanwhile, some turn to apathy, not as a passive retreat, but as a conscious revolt against complexities that can no longer be handled.

The metaphor for our age may someday be found in some hellish landscape such as that at Verdun, where for a year men fought over and over and over again for the same few inches of ground, paying half a million lives neither to gain nor to lose. We are sometimes afraid of all our sorrows, present and yet to come. Sometimes we're pretty sure everything is going to clog up, run down, or give out.

The items on a list of lamentations might be multiplied again and again. Indeed, I'm moved to question the judgment of anyone who is not occasionally disturbed, confused, alarmed. I don't think about such things all of the time, but hearing about them does make the mower heavier and the mowing harder. It does make the life in the grass seem empty of hope. Truly, as Maynard Mack has remarked, "to the wretched, all weather is wintry."

And yet, failure and woe need not be ultimate facts of life. Our past, even if it sometimes seems to have brought us to a sorry, woeful condition, has held dear and precious things—good houses, full of sweet people, some long since gone; good coffee, though now we'll have to learn to plant a better crop; good country, much of it now paved; good music, dimly heard in the cacophony and turmoil of change.

Besides, we were not promised that the earth would come of age in us. We were not promised that change would cease when it reached our house. All of creation may yet groan and lurch up out of itself, and we can go into a new world clasping to our memories what was dear in the old. Strange and marvelous things have happened before. If doom seems sometimes to hang down about us, marvels also wait upon us.

Consider one particular marvel: every plant that sustains us used to be a weed. Yet in time weed became food, and in the process we became other than what we had been. Consider, for example, the black-eyed pea. Cultivated in antiquity, from origins

in Africa, the plant spread to the Mediterranean countries, and the Greeks and Romans knew it. Taken by the Spanish into the West Indies in the sixteenth century, it was established on this continent by the eighteenth century. The dried seeds of the black-eyed pea, *Vigna sinensis,* may be ground into meal for various uses, or taken as a coffee substitute. "The fresh seeds and immature pods," one source remarks, "may be eaten." That seems scant justice: black-eyed peas, especially in the company of onions and corn bread, are a staple of Southern diets, a necessity to the sustenance of a meager life, a delicacy to the palate of the knowing eater. Yet another writer, not given to Southern ways, says the *Vigna sinensis* is grown in warm regions for green manure and forage.

The turnip, *Brassica napus,* is the civilized kin of *Brassica campestris,* which grows wild in sandy soils, originally and prolifically near the seaside in northern Europe, whence it came to be a chief source of food, filling though of no great nutritional value, to early Gallic, Germanic, and Celtic peoples. It remained a staple until the late medieval period, when it lost out to the potato, and dwindled into the present, when it is oftener remembered not for its taste but for its lack of blood. Even now, it has not lost its close similarity to the natural growth, the weed *Brassica campestris,* that grows near northern seashores.

Ipomea batatas, the sweet potato, is sister to the morning glory. Common enough in most warm areas of the world, it is forsaken in some because of the great, long, trailing, space-usurping vines of its maturity. Apparently it came to these western continents from the East by way of Polynesia. Not all of its history was lost in the strange voyage: a Peruvian dialect calls the potato *cumar,* a Polynesian dialect calls it *kumara,* and a Maori dialect calls it *umara.* However it came to these shores, it came early; a word for the potato occurs in many early dialects of Peru, the Yucatan, the Caribbean islands. The word of San Domingo, *batata,* corrupted by Englishmen, gave us our word, potato. Columbus took plantings back to Europe from his first voyage. Now it is most commonly found in bins and piles at the grocery store, and some say it's attractive under brown sugar, molasses, and marshmallows, but it's still the sister to the natural morning glory.

The wild version of *Raphanus sativus,* our radish, is *Raphanus raphanistrum,* and the two are scarcely distinguishable. The radish has a long history, but it has not lost its connection with weeds. There is a mention of radish in China in 1100 B.C. Herodotus tells of an inscription he saw in Egypt which proclaimed that the builders of the Great Pyramid ate prodigious amounts of radish—perhaps it had already won its reputation for curative and generative powers. Anglo-Saxons in later centuries used the radish in recipes against madness, demonic temptation, and possession. It also occurred in poultices and drinks for headaches, pains in the joints, eyeaches, and warts. Withal it manages to be fetching when eaten raw, especially when it is coldly crisp. But the round-red radish, lying coolly in a bed of lettuce on the relish tray served smartly at your local restaurant, is not significantly different from *Raphanus raphanistrum,* the weed radish.

All of these—black-eyed peas, turnips, sweet potatoes, radishes —are growing now in our garden against the coming of frost. So, too, are okra, which takes its name from *nkruma,* its name in the Tshi language of Ghana; brussels sprouts, whose origins are unknown, though it has been of latter centuries common in Belgium, whence its name; and onions, kin to the lily, common in

Egyptian tomb paintings, unfit for Brahmins and yoga practition-
ers, object of fond recollection for wilderness Jews (see Numbers
11:5—when they remembered Egypt, it was for "the cucumbers
and the melons, and the leeks and the onions and the garlic").

All of them once were weeds, natural growths, thought useless.

Somewhere, sometime, perhaps along a lonesome stretch of
the Nile in a time none can chronicle, a weed stretched and cast
its spores into the wind, one to become a lily, another to become
an onion, only to wait another eon before someone discovered
it was edible. And elsewhere, in a cool, unknown place, a cab-
bage weed exercised itself and became brussels sprouts. Elsewhere
still, southerly, deep in Africa, someone saw the beasts eat okra
weed and found that it was good. Someone cold and afraid of his
hunger knelt near the sea along what would one day be a Danish
shore, dug a strange root, ate, survived, and a weed became a
turnip.

All of them once were weeds, natural growths, thought useless.

Some are weeds still and useless still to parts of humankind.
In some provinces black-eyed peas are not tolerable as food. To
those who don't fancy pot likker, turnip greens are less tasteful
than poor grass, and the turnip itself seems merely a root. The
radish is to even discriminating eyes much like the wild members of its family.

All of them once were weeds, natural growths, thought useless.
Everything used to be a weed. All that became, became from
weeds. Some things, like the turnip, may yet become weeds again.

And if all of them once were weeds, if everything used to be
a weed, may we not, with some reason, wait and watch with glad
surmise, dig strange roots, prune alien plants to fuller growth,
discover that what is now a weed may yet be fruit, and all be fed?

Surely so. Such marvels do occur. But they need our making.

That brings me back to the lawn where I started. Unattended,
my lawn would be a weedy lot eight weeks from now. Everything
that was a weed will go back to weed if it is not clipped and mowed
and cultivated, and no casual cutting will do. What was alien weed
must be trimmed to fuller growth, manured by work and pruned
by art. Just so are marvels made; just so are new worlds found
and learned. The imagination, Whitehead has reminded us, has
contagious power to construct new visions, to rekindle zest.

41

The ritual of today can free the mind to consider the possibilities of tomorrow. Thoughtless, hurried cutting won't do. Priesting to the lawn is no casual art. You don't just whir up the mower and go tearing across the grass catty-cornered or zig-zag. That's not the way at all. Oh, you can do it helter-skelter if you please, mow plaids, play X's and O's in the grass, if you're of a mind to. But that's not the way. Priesting to the lawn has its mysteries and rituals, has its proper liturgy.

We have two lawns to do, contiguous, ours and the widow lady's next door to the north. First, I mow the small north side of her lawn, and it must be done in decreasing rectangles. Then come the front slopes of both lawns, back and forth, neatly overlapping. The slopes done, I strain and heave the mower back up to the big flat area of our adjoining yards. That has to be done in diminishing ells, with one stop to trim around the red bud tree. There's little more: a quick strip down our south side, then diminishing squares do the last flat of the south yard, with genuflections at the elm, the mulberry, and the sweet gum tree. I've neglected to mention six or ten stops for the drinking of holy water and a general sagging.

Now there is some consequence to this ministry. It gets the lawn mowed—pretty clean, mostly even. Sometimes it mainly makes me sweat. Sometimes, my mind vacated, the ritual removing all need to think on mowing, I compose sharp REBUTTALS FOR USE IN DAY-OLD CONVERSATIONS. Sometimes, images of grief fill up the unused space in my mind, and I run behind the mower to shake them loose. Sometimes, I'm pretty sure the liturgy signifies nothing; other times, near the end, when I'm hot and the lawn mower is pushing back, I conclude that I'm caught in obsession, unable to mow another pattern.

But sometimes, maybe for a moment or two out of one mowing per summer, I think I get a sign and learn what liturgy is for, working back in my mind to the word's original signification of both public worship and public work, this last in the sense of a public duty a citizen is obliged to meet.

Seven years ago I mowed a different pattern. Three years ago I mowed another. Now I've learned this way, *the* way. Each pattern got the lawn mowed. Each kept leg and eye and arm fixed to need. Now my sense of the slope and tilt of the yard and the bend of the grass and my sense of my own duration have taught me this way. And that's what liturgy is for: it gets the service done while we learn another way to name and know and locate God.

Over in our secular world, that's how marvels are made, how alien weeds become filling fruits, how new worlds are found. To the bitter weeds, the grinding losses, the searing terrors of the world, we bring the manuring of our work, the pruning of our art. We cannot go on being what we have always been. If we settle for that, we settle for weeds and woe. We can, instead, make a liturgy that will get done what needs doing. Sustained by that liturgy, while the work gets done, we can learn to reach out and enfold creation, making thereby new liturgies of life and regeneration. And then we shall not be afraid of the terror that comes by night or of the arrow that flies by day.

A Snake in the Garden at John Graves's Place

Moses, Milton, and the Lord God Almighty made a good plan and worked it well, seemed to know the way the world and all would wobble, and me, giving Satan a snake's skin, that time in the garden.

We were at Graves's place, early, before his house was finished, and everything was mighty noble and to my great content. We drove with kids and friends beyond Mrs. Crockett's grave, down past the dog-run cabin, past Glen Rose, along the Paluxy to the flat rock bed where the river runs thin. Downriver great flat boulders leaned, broken from shelving earth in some surprising saurian time. And then we drove up the narrow road, weeds levering against the car, into the creek bed, past the hogs, up, and through his gate.

It was a hundred and forty acres, scrub and creek and mountain. We sat in the blue shade of his porch, sawdusted from his work, and touched the blue-streaked lintel stones, and fingered stones he'd built into his walls from forgotten houses, some still marked with a mason's chisel of a style not used for ninety years. We walked his fence line, found his mountain, set it aside for fall when the brush would die back. We named the trees as best we could, hunted birds, saw a thresher, and all things mighty noble.

Then we saw the snake, somnolent, but coiled and there. I walked by, and the girls, and the boy would have stepped in the very coil but my wife saw and eased him back, and then adrenaline drain and green gall and cotton spit and quietness came over us all, and we watched for no more birds, but doubted every step.

Later, with a Thermos and Viennas, sitting on the smooth rock bed of the creek beside the water above his little fall, the boy skipping flat rocks, the girls watching twigs drop over the fall and twist and dance, later, that is, we breathed and remembered that snakes *do* live in Texas. Then we could relax and hear the hoot a long way off, hear the water twirling and curling over the fall, hear the flat rocks skipping over the water.

And then it was, had already become, another snake story. When I told my father—we were leaning on the table, sipping the sweet cold tea at the bottom of the last glass—my mother, hearing, fretted the dishes around us and dreaded the snake that already was. Then my father told me, perhaps again, how he and Uncle Bill stirred up a bunch of rattlers resting on the front porch of their den, how they killed some and then thought they'd need a gun to get the rest, and how he lit out for the house and looked down from the air in his second stride and saw a snake where he wanted to land and so changed directions while he was still up there.

And he told, again, about how Uncle Jack, when he still had both his legs, stepped on a rattler and surprised them both and later laughed and told the boys how he hit at that snake nine times before he came down the first time.

And he told, again, about how my grandfather, when he was just a father and thought it was just a garden snake, went into the grape arbor with a rake to kill a snake the kids had seen, about how when he got in there it was a rattler and he hit it with a rake and got it on the tines and, thinking it dead, put the rake over his shoulder to carry the snake off, about how he looked around to see the snake still alive and twisting at him from around the tines, and how thinking about the little dance he did then the boys would laugh sometimes when he wasn't looking and sometimes when he was.

And he told, again, about how when he was a boy he had a friend who had a brother who was slow-witted, how the friend, hoeing cotton, saw the rattler around his brother's feet two rows away and knew he could not speak because the snake would strike sooner than the brother would move, and so with no word knocked his brother, not quite bright, from off the snake, and how the brother chased him with his hoe clear out of the field and past the barn and to the house and never knew the snake had coiled around his feet.

Surprising and sweet and sad, how they were real before I knew them.

Moses and Milton and the Lord God Almighty made a good plan and worked it well, seemed to know the way the world and all would wobble, and me, giving Satan a snake's skin, that time in the garden. How sweet and sad and still surprising, they were all real before I knew them. Uncle Jack and the Grandfather and the brother all got real, came into my mind, when the snake coiled. I learned after silence and the dread of time to hear the hoot a long way off and the water twisting and curling over the fall and the sound of flat rocks skipping over the water, and after a while I began to wonder if there has to be a snake to make our garden.

Featured on Today's Menu: Desperation, with a Mayonnaise of Longing and Regret

Sometimes I go to the delicatessen not to get anything, but to read the labels on cans and jars, thinking maybe I'll learn something mysterious and wonderful or find out how things are in Prague or Budapest or Odessa. I always read the food column in the *New York Times Magazine* on Sundays, and I read recipes in the local newspaper—the special food section, every Thursday morning—and in magazines I chance upon here and there. Whenever I learn about a grocery store, say Chicotsky's on Bellaire, for example, that carries "gourmet" foods or ethnic specialties or esoteric items, I try to get there and study the shelves, and often go back for further study sessions. I always expect that something magic is going to turn up, that something wonderful is going to happen. It mostly doesn't.

Still, I'm pretty excited when I learn how to prepare lamb chops with rosemary mayonnaise, or maybe chicken stuffed with chopped green onions and basted with butter, tarragon, and white wine, or perhaps a fish fillet with faint butter and lemon and pepper, or Croton Breaks cheese spread. And I get moderately stirred up when I stroll down the aisle of a grocery store and come upon antipasto di verdure, good peanut oil, six or eight different mustards, more varieties of pasta than even I had ever hoped to see, Vidalia onion pickles, exotically stuffed olives (though none quite so exhilarating as those stuffed with jalapeños in San Angelo, Texas), Stilton, brie, havarti, diverse cheddars, paté with green peppercorns, and all the versions of fish that I only found I liked these latterly years. It's all astonishing to a fellow who never expected to see much beyond Kent County and a little piece of Dickens County, though on manic days I do claim that I have seen an elephant and heard the hoot owl cry.

I can't, you see, quite keep experience straight. I don't always know why I go looking for such things. Sometimes I think it's because there is such a multitude of things—foods, places, wonders—I didn't know about until I was grown. I expect young people now to know and to see and to taste, our technological expertise having made very nearly everything accessible and available, so that a city deep in the interior can have a pretty good seafood restaurant, for example. I expect the youngsters to know about things I didn't know about when I was young; but I find that many people of my generation, all those who grew up in some elsewhere, also knew early on about much that I didn't know until later. I remember one episode of catfish and one of fried oysters when I was young, but otherwise I didn't eat seafood until well after I was grown, and I don't think I knew what a shrimp looked like until after I was out of high school. I didn't eat—or see—cauliflower or asparagus or brussels sprouts or ravioli or most pastas or lasagna or mushrooms or any sausage except what was made from a hog at the farm or bean sprouts or

46

any Chinese food or any paté or most cheeses or most breads
other than biscuits and white bread or olives or artichokes or
Lord knows what else. A good many goods didn't reach Jayton
in the 1930s, freezing was unknown, and home refrigeration was
scarce. Diets were not exactly diverse. During World War II in
Fort Worth, people were mostly thinking about other things, using skills to other ends than the preparation and dispersal of
foods. Mostly, I know that what seems exotic and new and exciting to me, what looks like a "gourmet" item to me, is likelier
than not ordinary stuff to other folks. Sometimes I remember
that much of it is expensive and unnecessary, that to purchase
it is to be pretentious or precious. Nevertheless, I keep on looking: one day something special beyond special will turn up.

Like that one dear or splendid restaurant that I'll treasure for
the rest of my life. I'm obsessed by restaurants. I read the local
paper's listings and reviews in the special section on Thursday
morning and on Saturday morning, and mark places to go. I read
magazines, the *Texas Monthly*, for instance, that list and describe
restaurants in other Texas cities, and mark places to try if I ever
head out that way. When I travel, I read and note places to eat
in the cities where I find myself, and study the folders that you
sometimes find in hotel rooms. If I go to a conference or conven-
tion, I pore over the material the planners put in packets, looking for special restaurants. Sometimes I plan my days by meals
at this place or that, making sure to schedule all the places that
seem interesting. It's tiresome work, but I seem unable to avoid
it and imagine that each outing will lead to some grail.

I have, indeed, eaten at fine places. I remember Vincenzo, on
20th Street NW in Washington, and a wonderful Ethiopian restaurant across the Potomac, though I can't get its name back. I
remember Apley's in Boston, but the library's new Boston telephone book shows no such place. Even the good places come
and go, and I can't find some places again. I remember the Little
Rhein Steak House on South Alamo in San Antonio, and Tuffy's
in Galveston. I remember Jennivine's in Dallas, and Zentner's
Daughter in San Angelo, and Pulido's on Spring Street here at
home in Fort Worth, though it's not listed or reviewed, I guess,
because it's part of a chain of Mexican food restaurants. I also
remember the White Horse Inn in Rotterdam.

Even so, I can't keep experience straight. These, I think, were or are good restaurants with good food. But what is good to me is neither permanent nor ubiquitous; it is good generated by a time and a place and a mood and some food and some service and some company or some solitude. If someone asks me about a restaurant I've been to, about all I can manage to say is maybe, "Well, the time I ate there, it was really something special, or so it seemed to me." I'm always surprised to learn how easily some people—for instance, those who make lists and write descriptions and reviews of restaurants—seem to get things fixed in their minds, fixed, right by God, and forever. I can't get a hold on the good, or put a hold on the good. I keep wondering, trying to know, not making it, and looking for something wonderful to happen.

Mostly it doesn't, at least not in restaurants. I slowly begin to learn how bad most are (and bad is as much compounded of myself and my circumstances as good is). In even the most elegant and expensive, if there is oil, there is a suspicion too much, if there is seasoning, there is a wisp too much. Where there is cooking, there is often too much; there is, in general, some apparent unwillingness to trust to the nature of the food. Where there is fine interior design and elegant service, they sometimes compose a weighty sauce of pretense. A fellow really shouldn't have to listen to an altogether splendid waiter calling his meal a "presentation."

Indeed, I'm inclined now to think that the *real* junk food is that found, not in the godawful chain food places with rowdy signs, but in all those diverse restaurants that depend on precious manners or lively young waiters or wise older waiters or interesting decor or high prices or all of the above to persuade us that we are about to have something wonderful to eat, or that we have just had one of the world's great dining experiences. Not long ago I went into a restaurant (not the buffet, not the snack bar) in a major airport terminal. A lady welcomed me grandly, escorted me to a table, gave me a ponderous menu, and introduced me to my waiter, who a little later brought me food that could not have been so badly prepared without diligent practice. Not long ago I went to one of those fern-and-stained-glass-and-multiple-partition-and-cozy-central-bar restaurants that erupt spontaneously around the nation; the food I got looked great and tasted awful. Not long ago I went to a finely appointed restaurant in a Sheraton Hotel, a place very Englishy, with rafters and white linen and low lights and a dressing on the salad so heavy it mashed my taste buds. Not long ago I went to a popular, if expensive, restaurant here at home where an extensive and varied salad bar invited humans to be hogs, lining up at the pig trough to get so much salad that they would not notice the quality of their main course.

Better, perhaps, to go to McDonald's or Wendy's or Burger King or Dairy Queen and have some nondescript meat on inconsequential bread, and know that one wasn't getting much, and for less money.

Better, far, to do it oneself and cook with some care and delight.

But no, that won't do. There's always that awful hunger for imagined marvels, an emptiness of stomach and soul, a regret for what has passed, for what was around the corner that I didn't turn, a longing for what I might yet find. There's always a craving, a need to wait and to watch for something wonderful to happen.

History Is Fiction, except for the Parts That I Like, Which Are, of Course, True

I am not a historian, not a student of historical methodology or of historical criticism or of the writing of history. I am not able to make a responsible review of the literature for any particular field, subfield, or specific subject in history. It's unlikely, then, that I will be able to tell historians and students of history what they don't already know. I'll be glad if I can remind anyone present of what he or she already knows but may not have considered recently.

Though I am not, by the standards I have just suggested, qualified as a historian, I do hunger after accounts of whatever past can be known or accumulated for parts of West Texas. The scene I search is proportionately as limited as my qualifications. I have enjoyed the documents and histories of the area that lies west of Fort Worth and mostly north of Interstate 20. If pressed, I would, among the works I've enjoyed, cite especially Randolph Marcy's journals and reminiscences, Richardson's *The Frontier of Northwest Texas*, Hollon's *Beyond the Cross Timbers*, Williams's *The Big Ranch Country*, and Wallace's *Ranald Mackenzie on the Texas Frontier*, though there are others I might mention that are just as pleasurable to me. I have not found all I yearned for in these books. (We all, I suppose, yearn for the history we need.) The territory I love out there is not much chronicled. In what I have sometimes called the Big Empty, there are, perhaps, only small histories to tell, at least in modern times. Perhaps only the far past, still and perhaps forever hidden to us, holds tales that make learned papers and books.

I *do* qualify as a historian in one respect. All humans do. Each of us *is* a historian. Each of us accumulates evidence and insight, ignores some of it, fails to find other pieces, or chooses not to look. Each of us creates the history he or she can enjoy, or tolerate, or consider and turn away. Each of us forms a conception of the world, its institutions, its public, private, wide, or local histories. In this history making, as E. L. Doctorow says in his essay "False Documents," "there is no fiction or nonfiction as we commonly understand the distinction." There is only our making, sometimes by design, usually not. None of us lives without a history. We're always standing someplace in our lives, and there is always a history of how we came to stand there, though few of us have marked carefully the dimensions of the place where we are or the tale of how we came to be there.

The catch is that, though we are all historians, we cannot always be *good* historians. Sometimes we can't find all that's needed to make our history. Sometimes we don't see enough. Sometimes we find enough and see enough and still tell it wrong. Sometimes we fail to judge; sometimes we judge dogmatically, even ignorantly, only by standards we have already established. We see only what our eyes will let us see at a given time, but eventually make a history for ourselves that we can tolerate, or at least not have to think about too much (or else we don't, and have to be put away). Every so often, one of us will see something he or she or we have not seen before, and we have to remake our various histories. Some, however, will never see or hear any history but the one they've already made. We are always seeing, hearing, thinking, saying, and writing the fiction we and our time make possible and tolerable, a fiction, I will suggest, that is the history we can assent to at a given time. We not only cannot always be *good* historians, we cannot be *thorough* historians. We're always making fiction that always has to be remade, that is, unless we are so bound by arrogance, ignorance, or dogma that we cannot see a new artifact or hear a new view.

When I say that history is a fiction we make and sometimes remake, I do not mean that to be taken as an attack on historians and on their histories. I do not mean by saying this to minimize historical writing, or to call loud and obstreperous attention to the limitations of historians.

When I say that history is a fiction, I mean to identify a human condition, not an evil condition. (History as fiction may become evil if we refuse to see any history except the one we've already accepted or if we try to force that history on others.)

At any rate, making history as fiction is not by nature limited, valueless, ignorant, or despicable. It is human. It is what we do and what we are.

Language is what lets us be human. It is the great gift that lets us be what we are and hope to be, but even this great gift will not extend our capacities infinitely. Language comes out of us a word at a time; we cannot say everything at once. We have to open ourselves to experience and insight and evidence and say what we can, but what we say will invariably be incomplete. Two words cannot occupy the same space at the same time; two messages cannot occupy the same space at the same time. Language enforces a closure: we must say one thing or the other; we cannot get both said at the same time. To be sure, having spoken— or written—we can open ourselves again to experience and insight and evidence and try to say it all again. But what will come out will be fiction. We cannot make all that *was* into *is*. Whatever we can get into our heads we will make into a narrative that will be our truth until we learn again.

So there we are. We can't always be *good* historians. We usually can't be *thorough* historians. It follows, I think, that we cannot be *authoritative* historians. In a recent essay discussing the

views on history of Nietzsche and Michael Oakeshott ("Suppos-
ing History Is a Woman—What Then?" *American Scholar,* Au-
tumn, 1984), Gertrude Himmelfarb remarks that

> whatever "truth or validity" adheres to history . . . does not derive,
> as the conventional historian might assume, from an "objective"
> world, a world of past events waiting to be discovered and recon-
> structed by the historian. For there is no objective world, no histori-
> cal events independent of the experience of the historian, no events
> or facts which are not also ideas. "History is the historian's expe-
> rience. It is 'made' by nobody save the historian; to write history
> is the only way of making it." The function of the historian is to
> make coherent a multitude of past acts and events, and this coher-
> ence alone defines historical truth. (Internal quotation from Oake-
> shott, *Experience and Its Modes*)

The world and the events of its chronology look and act as
we ask them to look and act at a given time. Ask an electron
to act like a particle, and it will. Ask it to act like a wave, and
it will. Expect a band of Indians to number 2,500, and it probably
will. Under other circumstances, expect the band to number 150,
and it will. The human observer is a necessary link in any chain
of events. We are always an integral part of any process or event
being observed. The supposedly solid world we inhabit and seem
to grasp in our hands every day is, rather, a remarkably and almost endlessly varied gathering of visions. It surely seems, in the
latter part of the twentieth century, that it is at best difficult,
if not impossible, to say the final, authoritative word. It always
was, but we didn't always know it.

I have, nevertheless, longed at times to know *exactly* how
things were. I have sometimes thought that if I could just get
in the place where it happened and get myself situated just right
with the sun, then maybe I could really know what it was like
and how it looked with James Bowie in that little room, or with
Marcy when he traveled through the Croton Breaks and gave them
their name, or with Mackenzie when he stood looking out from
the headquarters porch at Fort Concho. Marcy and Mackenzie
almost certainly were in some places I wanted them to talk about,
but neither is specific enough at the right time to give me the
history I want. Neither had the grace to say what I wanted to

hear. I'll not get their sense of what it was like and how things looked.

We can't be final or authoritative. Sometimes too much is hidden from us, and our language is always inadequate, splendid as it can be at times.

If we can't be good, or thorough, or authoritative, then what enabling capacities can we hope for as fiction makers?

Well, there's not much I can say for sure. I'd guess that a responsible and enriching and bracing history is achieved when the writer is revealed as open to space and time, with all the histories contained there—big histories, little histories, big lies, little lies, old evidence, new evidence—and when the writer manages to keep all in harmony, not dropping old histories for new, but adding, adding, adding, knowing each history was right for a time, recognizing that it takes *all* histories to make history. We can learn from Henry James, William Faulkner, and others who have experimented with the use of shifting points of view, to keep looking in different places, to keep seeing with different eyes, sustaining and cherishing ambiguity and variety, adding, turning, looking again, holding all histories in harmony even while distinguishing among them.

We can't be final and authoritative; it may be that we cannot even be good. But we can be believable, trustable, evocative taletellers, if we can learn, as Himmelfarb suggests, "to dispense with absolute truth, to pursue . . . the reality of something only partially knowable." We can keep adding pieces here, rearranging pieces yonder, standing and turning our heads back to see how it looks elsewhere. "There is no history except as it is composed," Doctorow says, and the "act of composition can never end."

To illustrate more specifically what I've been trying to talk about, I want to take two passages from histories as focal points and tell about the trouble I have had in finding Fort Phantom Hill. I know where Fort Phantom Hill is—some ten or twelve miles northerly of Abilene, Texas—but that's not the same thing as finding it.

Before I had ever seen the ruins of Fort Phantom Hill, I had erected the fort many times in my mind.

Construction of the fort was authorized in November, 1851, by

General Order 91. Major General Smith, commanding the 8th Military Department, which included Texas, thought he was establishing a fort on the Clear Fork of the Brazos to protect settlers on the upper Brazos and Trinity rivers. The site, he was told, was "alive with deer, turkey, and bear." Truth was, the area lacked timber for construction, and water had to be hauled from four miles or so away. The fort, according to one story, took its name from a nervous sentry. One night during the first encampment, he fired at what he testified later was "an Indian on the hill." When no trace of the marauder could be found, the others concluded that it was a phantom—a phantom on the hill, hence Fort Phantom Hill. It's a grand name, full of wonder and romance, a name that might have resonated with sounds of heroism under desperate circumstances, a name scarcely matched by John Ford or John Wayne, or the makers of other cavalry fictions.

The fort, as it turned out, was not equal to the romance of its name. Not quite three years after it was established, it was abandoned, in April, 1854.

I had built Fort Phantom Hill long before from the lumber of a hundred movies, five hundred western fictions, and God knows how many cavalry stories, and I had peopled it with such folk as filled the pages of *Beau Geste*. When you're a boy and you live in another world and you haven't yet learned that war is wicked and ugly and that most of the games men play, in uniform and out, are at best foolish posturings, at worst forms of oppression —when you're a boy, I was about to say, a boy in such a world, a fort is a wondrous place where it is possible to be heroic.

54

Later, I learned about Fort Phantom Hill in other ways, in the first of two passages I want to cite, the words, written years later, of a lady who had lived at the fort as a girl. Mrs. Emma Johnson Elkins, writing in *Hunter's Magazine*, 1911, and quoted later by Carl Coke Rister and by Rupert Richardson, told how one day at the fort an alarm was sounded:

> The soldiers were soon in battle array. The whole tribe of Northern Comanches was coming in sight, the head chief Buffalo Hump in the lead, followed by his subordinates; then came the warriors, squaws, and papooses, 2500 in all. Seeing the preparation for their reception, it was too much for the noble red men and they passed on with scowls and angry looks, going in a westerly direction.

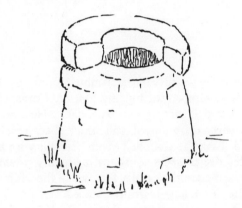

Later still I learned more—or rather, I learned to accept less of what I thought I had learned. Rupert Richardson, in *The Frontier of Northwest Texas*, suggested that for the sake of accuracy (in the second passage I want to cite) it would be a good idea "to divide the good old lady's 2500 by ten and subtract a hundred." He reckoned, in other words, that there could not have been more than about 150 in the Indian band.

And still later, I discovered that if there was heroism in this province, it didn't all belong to white people. On August 25, 1859, Major George Thomas and his cavalry troops came across a fresh Indian trail near Abilene. They followed it and finally sighted

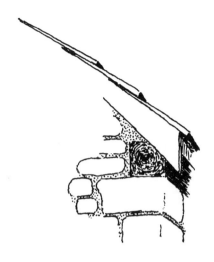

the Indians in the vicinity of the Double Mountains. The troops were clearly gaining on the Indians. One old Comanche warrior apparently decided that he was expendable. He dropped out of the Indian party, dismounted, and attacked the cavalry as they approached. Twice he wounded Major Thomas with his arrows. He wounded five troopers, all the while loudly cursing the cavalry. Then he died in the cavalry fire. But in the confusion of his delaying fire, his fellow warriors escaped.

Finally, I learned one more thing, which I've already mentioned. I had pictured Fort Phantom Hill in my mind along with the others — Fort Richardson, Fort Griffin, Fort Concho, and the rest — and had conceived them as, if not permanent, at least durable, continuously present in the landscapes of fantasy where warfare might be noble and men might be brave. But then I learned it was all a mistake: the army goofed and built the fort in the wrong place; there was no timber; there was scant water; and the fort itself was occupied for only three years.

Perhaps you will understand, then, that when I finally did go and actually see the ruins of Fort Phantom Hill, I didn't know which Fort Phantom Hill to look at. I didn't know which Fort Phantom Hill was real. Was I to look at the fort of my old imag-

inings and picture myself bravely at its ramparts? Was I to see the small, beleaguered but noble band of troops in that old lady's fort? To her, as a small girl, the force of the Comanches' presence must have seemed 2,500, regardless of later judgments. Was I to try to see the fort as Buffalo Hump saw it? Was I to see the sane and sober historian's fort? Was I only to see the small ruins of an old mistake? I stood there a while that morning, and after a bit I came away.

It's hard to find Fort Phantom Hill. You won't find it if you look from a single viewpoint, imprisoned by a single, narrow vision. I do not want to accept a single vision of our work, however well it may be documented. The prospect seems perilous to me, and sad.

Must I learn to see Fort Phantom Hill in only one way? Must I see forever only the small and scattered ruins that I saw that morning? Must I give up seeing it as that old lady saw it, remembering her girlhood, when a company of troopers stood against the odds? Yet if I see it only in her way, I surrender the power to see it as the historian sees it. Must I forget the dream fort I

erected before I ever saw Fort Phantom Hill? Must I cease trying to see it as Buffalo Hump saw it? I choose not to.

I declare instead that we must be full of many visions. There is much about me that might be corrected, but I don't have to give up any of my versions of Fort Phantom Hill. I can keep them all. I don't have to look at the fort in a single way. I treasure each way of looking; each fiction teaches me something precious and dear. Remember, please, that we are complex, not simple. We must ransack all human experience for its good, and hold many a vision dear.

Bad ideas and single visions require civil and loving correction, else we become victims and servants, subjects to whatever someone tells us, subjects to our own uninformed fancies. That fantasy fort I imagined as a boy is dear to me, but it is not Fort

Phantom Hill. That old lady's remembrance of the place is sweet and right, but it does not tell the whole truth. I have to read the historian's account. I have to try to see it as Buffalo Hump saw it. I have to go and see the ruins. I have to keep looking. Fort Phantom Hill exists and has its identity in all of the versions of it that we know or may yet make, in all our fictions.

Lieutenant T. L. Chadbourne, 1822–46

About halfway down Highway 277 from Abilene to San Angelo, on a low bluff above the road on the left, there is a marker, just about all the evidence left of Fort Chadbourne.

The fort was established in 1852 by units of the Eighth United States Infantry, and was also a station on the Butterfield stage and mail line. The State of Texas took it over as the Civil War was beginning. United States troops occupied it for a short while after the war, but then Chadbourne gave way to the new Fort Concho down the road in San Angelo. Concho had better water, and it put troops nearer where they were needed. Now the marker is about all that's left of Fort Chadbourne.

But during the 1850s, life was active enough there. A band of Comanches stole a small herd of horses while passengers on the Butterfield stage were watching. A Captain Van Buren was killed nearby in 1854. Comanches took two military mail carriers, tied them to a tree, and burned them. Rupert N. Richardson tells of a soldier "who after an attack by Indians managed to get into the post, even though he had fourteen arrows in him and bristled like a porcupine. A doctor removed the arrows, and within two weeks the soldier was walking around." Richardson also tells of nonviolent times:

> Happily not all relations between the races at Fort Chadbourne had to do with tomahawk and rifle. When the wife of Dr. Ebenezer Swift, the post surgeon, gave birth to a baby boy the squaws formed a line to see the white baby. "Chiquito Medico," Little Doctor, they called the child. (Many Texas Comanches spoke a little Spanish.) In *Our Wild Indians*, Colonel Richard M. Dodge, who knew the Old West from experience, attaches to Fort Chadbourne a tale told

all along the Great Plains frontier. Indians were fond of horse-racing and gambling and not infrequently officers and troops at frontier posts would match them. Mu-la-que-top, a Comanche, matched with an officer at the fort a race in which the Indian's sheep-like pony bested a fine Kentucky mare belonging to the officer. The red man added insult to financial injury by riding the last fifty yards of the race face to tail, beckoning the rider of the mare to come on.

Fort Chadbourne was named for Lieutenant Theodore L. Chadbourne, who, not long out of West Point, was with Zachary Taylor's army not too far from Brownsville. Lieutenant Chadbourne was born at Eastport, Maine, on August 2, 1822. He graduated West Point on July 1, 1843, a brevet second lieutenant, and spent two years at Fort Niagara. Then he was promoted to second lieutenant and assigned to the Eighth Infantry in the Military Occupation of Texas. He fought in the Battle of Palo Alto on May 8, 1846. He was killed the next day in the Battle of Resaca de la Palma, on May 9, 1846. A register of West Point graduates shows that Theodore Lincoln Chadbourne was fifteenth in the class of 1843. When he died at Resaca de la Palma, he was still twenty-three. U.S. Grant was twenty-first in the same class. Otherwise, I can't find him; nothing tells me much. He didn't make it to the *Dictionary of American Biography*.

On down the road, in San Angelo, there are other traces. One of the main streets in the city is Chadbourne Street. Maybe it, too, was named for him. Maybe it was named, instead, for the fort.

His tunic hangs in a glass case in the museum that is in the headquarters building of old Fort Concho. A white strap hangs down from the right shoulder, across the chest, to the waist on the left, where the sword would hang. In the center of the strap, over the heart, there is a neat bullet hole. He was young, still twenty-three, and a long way from home, though young men have died in farther places.

I have stood more than once before that case and wondered how it was with him. I have wondered how and when his family came to know that he had been killed. Friends in the History Department where I teach tell me that they can only make guesses about how the word got back home. Perhaps by courier to a boat waiting at the mouth of the Rio Grande, one says, then to New Orleans to a mail boat to New York, then slow post to

Maine. I guess his family still lived in Eastport: the museum has a photograph of the family home there, taken around the turn of the century. Another friend suggests that messages maybe had to go by courier all the way to Galveston, then by boat to New Orleans, or direct to New York. Both say it must have taken two months, maybe a little less, maybe a lot longer.

What's it like, I have wondered, to learn that you have hovered in anxiety over a young man's welfare, worried about him, held him in your mind, prayed for him, long after he was dead? It must be unspeakably hard for a family.

But harder, I expect, to be a young man, probably hot that May 9, 1846, probably tired, maybe dirty, maybe scared, certainly dead, at twenty-three.

Can Poetry, or Water, Be Found in West Texas?

A while back, I talked about my province, which is a cosmos. Its outer dimensions, you may conclude, are a little narrow, though its middle is wide and various. I'm undisturbed about being provincial: this province is the nearest thing I've got to what Judith Wright calls "my blood's country."

Much of it has been and will be desert. The desert tends to win on all planets, and that's undisturbing, too. It saves one from some delusions. We were not, and the desert was. After a while, we will not be, and the desert will remain.

I should make it clear, however, that I'm not really willing or wanting to *recommend* provincialism; yet I do want to find writers who know, display, and create the province, lifting it in its very ordinariness to its whole accessible meaning. I'm not altogether content with the established sacred canon of literature, though I cherish some of the texts just this side idolatry. I want to find writers of and about this province who will see, marvel at, and praise small things—the ordinary heroes and heroines of our lives, the lonesome landscapes, the sweet, quirky, unhonored people who make the world go, a world full of grace, sadness, lunacy, and joy.

I want to try to say why I'm not always content with the great books that recur in our curricula. Perhaps the Double Mountains both require and generate a different inspiriting from that found at Parnassus.

The first book I ever owned was *Andy at Yale*, by Roy Eliot Stokes, published in 1914, though I didn't come to own it until maybe 1937. I learned a good many things from this book. I learned that there are such things as colleges (and probably, by the way, acquired from it an idealized view of college that has made every campus I've known seem a disappointing failure). I learned that men prove themselves on the football field and the baseball diamond. Andy returns to the huddle at one point, "panting, trembling, with a wild, eager rage to again get into the fight." I learned that men don't cringe or cry. "Keep quiet," the hero tells the villain, "for the honor of Yale whose name you've disgraced." These lessons were brought home to me again by *Fighting Blood*, a second book, whose author I've forgotten.

Meanwhile, I had been learning lessons secondhand through my brother. He was five years older and given to sophisticated ways. Whenever possible, he read pulp magazines filled with flying stories. In 1938, the only good war writers had to write about was World War I, and the stories were all about flying aces of 1917 and 1918. I learned lessons from them, too. I learned that good men are brave, that they are likely to be either stoic or flippant or wry in the face of danger or pain, that war is an appropriate form of human behavior, that it is a final testing ground for manhood.

And while this was going on, I was learning how to define the world, how to behave, how to measure myself, how to measure others from Tom Mix, Hoot Gibson, Ken Maynard, Buck Jones, later from Hopalong Cassidy, Gary Cooper, Sam Spade, and the sportswriters' versions of Joe DiMaggio.

When I got to be ten or eleven, I discovered P. C. Wren's *Beau Geste* and Baroness Orczy's *The Scarlet Pimpernel* and learned how to be valorous. I learned that struggle, usually physical, was the male mode, that physical dexterity and prowess were required, that the milder arts of meditation seldom registered, that decisiveness was better than thorough contemplation. I learned again that war was a proper arena for men, and I learned that women were nice but nonvital adornments to a male world.

Later, I set out on the road to Parnassus, went to college, and took English courses. I read *Beowulf* and learned what a hero is. He is male. He is white. He is active. He performs prodigious physical deeds. He is very much like a good linebacker. I read Chaucer and saw the large dimensions of that male world. You'll mention, perhaps, the Wife of Bath, but she is striking, after all, largely because she talks like a man. I read *Sir Gawain and the Green Knight* and learned that women have some uses, but only as testing agents for men. I was on the road to Parnassus, but I wasn't getting there.

I learned that we prized epic, tragedy, and romance as media for expressing our best selves. I learned what kind of people get to appear in epic, tragedy, and romance. Meanwhile, the newspapers, radio, and television were writing, speaking, and filming the first scriptures in our religion of athletics, teaching men that the best were those of whom it could be said, "He's some kind of football player," "He really knows how to hit," "He's reckless when he comes down that field," "When he hits you, you stay hit."

I read Byron, Shelley, and Keats and learned more lessons. I learned what it takes to be a poet: you need to be a man; you need to be restless and reckless and to use up women; or if you can't manage that, you need to die young. Later, I learned from others that you also need to drink a lot. I read Faulkner and Hemingway and learned how to be a novelist. It requires hunting, fishing, more drinking, and other male pursuits. I was on the road to Parnassus, but somehow I wasn't getting there.

One day I noticed that I wasn't sure I should make the trip. One day I noticed that what I had learned was not, perhaps, what I should have learned or might have learned. I had learned that the world was male, that the males were white, that they behaved according to values developed in physical conflict, that their appropriate testing was in warfare or some suitable conflict. I noticed, too, that the males were oftener than not privileged—they held power and place in one way or another.

And so one day I noticed something else. I noticed that the people I loved would not qualify for the world defined in those books along the road to Parnassus. Epic, tragedy, and romance would not admit many I loved.

And I was angry. I am a little angry still.

Why, when we defined heroism, did we exclude, for example, my father and mother? Why are the sweet, zesty, gentle, cantankerous people of our lives excluded from those books?

My father never struck anyone, never competed in sports, never went to war. He has, I think, always wanted to be defined to us in the ways the world has taught us, but he doesn't qualify. He is gentle, kind, selfless, patient, and mostly poor, in his earlier days at least. Yet when we were all younger, I remember seeing him work until he dropped for my mother, my brother, and me. He has never known that he counted; the world, after all, honors other kinds of men.

My mother is an extraordinary mix—acutely shy, yet at the same time just about the fastest in the west when it comes to puncturing a swollen ego. A model of natural dignity and reserve, she is not beautiful and brilliant as the world reckons such things. The world honors other kinds.

However, I didn't set out to tell you about my parents. You have your *own* problems, after all. I select them because I know them. They got left out of all those books along the old road to Parnassus. Anyone could furnish scores and scores of others similarly excluded.

I'd not want to be misunderstood. I do not wish to repudiate the literature of the past. The past is in us, inescapably; if we repudiate the past, we deny ourselves. The past is in us. We can love it, even in its errors, and cherish what we were. The past calls out to us, "Remember. Remember."

But if we are not to repudiate the past, neither are we to accept it uncritically or to teach it unthinkingly. North of Delphi, Parnassus rises 8,061 feet; it was the home of the muses. The Castalian Spring there was the source of poetic inspiration. But remember, too, that Parnassus is also a barren limestone mass.

Those muses prompted and that inspiration generated beautiful songs, grand and moving stories, compelling visions. Without them we'd be bitterly poor and strangers to the truth. But they left out altogether some dear people and some dear places.

Instead of the precious, wonderfully uninteresting, but, oh my, marvelously knowledgeable poetry favored by many contemporary journals, instead of the generally self-serving and incestuous poetry issuing from many East Coast publishers, I'd like to

hear something different. I want to hear about such folks as my
father and how he knows how to make cement, not by recipe,
but by something in his bones. I want to hear how my grandfather
learned to plow a straight furrow and why even older men always
called him Mister. I want to know all of the reasons why, those
years ago, my mother cried when the tomatoes in her garden
twisted and died.

I want to know—to hear some singer sing—the names of bush,
tree, vine, weed, and what toll it takes when the wind comes
up across the plains, whipping the dust along.

I want to know what it was like for the Comanches when they
looked up one morning in Palo Duro Canyon and saw that the
world was over. The Holocaust and the Diaspora occur time and
time again, but we don't stop to notice.

I want to know the taste of water bought by the dirty barrel
load to refill the cistern when the rain doesn't come, and what
it's like to see boll weevils take a whole year's crop in a few days.

I want to hear some singer sing whether it's true—as my
mother said—that mockingbirds talk to cardinals, and that's how
word gets around that winter is gone.

I want to hear some singer sing whether it's true that, although
the doctors diagnosed cancer, Aunt Bertha really died of a dust
storm in her belly.

I want to know—to hear some singer sing—how it was for our
aunts, who took their first teaching jobs, living in dingy farmhouses with the families whose children they taught—imagine
them alone, in lonesome country far from home, with only one
smoky kerosene lamp against the dark, and the wind whistling
and moaning against the window.

I want some singer to sing how it was for our fathers to do
grinding, back-breaking work for two dollars a day.

I want to know what it means to be taught—or at least to learn,
if not to be taught—a frivolous and foolish version of what is
manly and durable, and how to give up that imagery when it is
time to do so. Some time ago, I read in the newspaper that Ken
Maynard had died. It caused a considerable depression, and I had
to postpone hoeing the garden. Lou Gehrig was long since dead.
Babe Ruth was long since dead. And now the last of the *big four*
was dead. Tom Mix died in 1940 in a car wreck. Buck Jones died

in 1942 in a fire at the Coconut Grove. Hoot Gibson died in 1966 of cancer. And now Ken Maynard was dead at 77. He made some three hundred movies, earning as much as eight thousand dollars a week, but he died in a small house trailer, alone, of physical deterioration and malnutrition. The last of the big four was gone, few heroes are left, and when your household gods are not re-generative, it's lonesome when they die.

I want to hear some singer sing about the variously sweet and mean people who live in Spur. At its peak, Spur, Texas, had a population of about three thousand. It lies off the main route between Fort Worth and Lubbock in a county that in many years has the lowest per capita income in the state. I used to go back to Spur from time to time, but now the last of my people there are gone. Some years ago my grandfather died; then soon his farm-house burned. About a year later my definite aunt and my gentle uncle moved away to the city. Once my people were scattered all over that county and the next. Now they are gone. The wind passes over the places where they were, and they are gone, and the places where they were will know them no more. I don't go back to Spur anymore. Of the few that are left, there's none I know.

If to long for such things is provincial, if to long to hear a singer singing such songs is provincial, then I am provincial, and largely undisturbed about it.

But a fellow really needs to be careful about what he hopes for, asks for. Sometimes he gets it, and sometimes it's what he wanted, and sometimes it isn't.

The Texas Water Development Board's plans may tell what I mean.

The Board presented an aggressive program at a public meet-ing in Lubbock in June, 1966. Themes and variations have been played since, and have recently been in the news again. Among them is one that particularly struck me.

Given the failing water supply across West Texas, given the waning resources of the Ogallala Aquifer, some have proposed a massive importation of water into West Texas from out of state. That seems sweet and reasonable, meant for the salvation of my province. Specifically, according to one plan, a canal would be dug from the Mississippi more or less straight across North Texas just north of Fort Worth, along the watershed between the Trinity and Red River basins, on to the divide between the Brazos and Red rivers, and on to White River Canyon. The map I saw once shows the canal going directly through—and destroying—the cosmos I have tried to describe. That's no longer sweet and reasonable.

I don't know whether that plan—or another like it—will work. I hope it doesn't, and I hope it does. I wanted my territory saved, somehow, but I guess I wanted it to be saved in my way. Another may come and find an order in it, or impose an order upon it, that I had not imagined. That canal wants to save and create life, too, though not mine. If I want to be sad because I can't find and keep the West Texas I imagined *and* learn the other that someone else imagined, that's my problem, a serious flaw in my character, but not something that should cause worry. Good writing might yet save both for me, and I hope I can celebrate. The desert leaves no delusions about abundant life going on after us: the desert tends to win on all planets. But good writing saves, renews, re-creates it all, and that may require the enactment of the Brazos, the Croton Breaks, and that dreadful, straight-sided canal. It may be that there will be no ultimate singer for that old cosmos I thought I knew, but there's nothing out there, as it was, as it will be, to prevent that singer's singing.

As It Turns Out, I'm Not Thoreau

My mother has never been given to crying. I don't know that she ever actually catechized me just so, but I somehow learned from her that you're not supposed to make scenes. I learned that, even if I don't always live that way.

At any rate, I was startled the first time I remember seeing her cry. I don't know when it was—maybe summer, 1937. We lived in the little house on the rim of the first canyon in the Croton Breaks, next door to the Lowrances. She had put in a garden that spring, but neither the garden nor anything else did all that well. The winds came, and the dust, and the sky went copper and red and brown and purple and black, and the temperature rose. The black-eyed peas came up, as I remember, and did middling well, but her little tomato plants withered and died. That's when she cried. I understand now better than I did then. I came to understand even better in the summer of 1980, when I stopped gardening.

Most people who lived through the summer in this territory have something to say about the rigors of heat and drought. I saw a bumper sticker the other day that said, "I Lived through the Summer of '80," and I understand that T-shirts are available proclaiming the same message. By the time this is in print, perhaps we'll all be able to look back on this startling summer with wry nostalgia. Right now, I don't feel particularly reflective: it's still dry and I'm still hot.

But I had started to say why I stopped gardening. I think I know the advantages of gardening. Since I began years ago, we've had herbs (which I grew more to look at than to use), tomatoes, peppers, onions, okra, radishes, green beans, black-eyed peas, turnips, squash, Jerusalem artichokes—a little dab of some, a lot of others. That's advantage enough. The black-eyed peas alone, when touched up with some onions and backed with a little cornbread, would make gardening worthwhile.

And there are other advantages: the seeding and weeding that are perpetually necessary tend to keep a gardener in the posture for prayer, which I characteristically need.

But I had started to say why I stopped gardening. A garden plot some thirty feet by sixty feet could and should produce considerable amounts of food. I don't know that there is a single reason why I gave that up. I'm going to chronicle various reasons, and quit when I think I've justified stopping.

I had gardened for several years when, a few years ago, gardening suddenly became popular here in the city. Then I worried some about gardening, fearing that someone would think I was being faddish. When bicycling became popular a few years ago, I nearly gave up the bicycle that I've ridden to work for fifteen years for that same reason. It's not in keeping with one's status as an intellectual, you know, to be caught doing something that is popular. Nevertheless, I went on riding my bicycle, and I went on gardening.

My own ineptitude kept eroding my hopes for abundance. Even when the crops were decent, they weren't enough to provide good meals the winter through. I expect all of us always hope for plenitude of some kind, whether in goods, pleasures, or freedoms. I don't particularly want a yacht or twenty-seven credit cards, or a bigger house or a longer car. I do want lots of coffee, with piles of sugar in it, and plenty of good pipe tobacco. The garden kept interfering with this dream of plenitude. The stubbornness of the soil and the chanciness of the weather kept teaching me that plenitude might not be within my reach and, worse, it might be the wrong dream.

It was hot. I have notes from several seasons I gardened. They record temperatures and rainfall and note planting dates. As the summer of 1980 progressed, the records became more sporadic: the sparse, bleak notations of life at the edge of the Great American Desert.

The garden kept me too well acquainted with my own mortality, and a fellow can tolerate only so much of that. At the outset of each season, when the soil had to be turned and fertilized and mulched, I hurt for three or four weeks, sometimes, I was sure, approaching death or a permanent crippling. Thereafter, minor lacerations and contusions, together with a fairly constant soreness, reminded me that I wasn't the man I used to be—and probably never had been.

It was still hot. By June the ground had the aspect of adobe.

One has to add a touch of laziness to the list. I wasn't diligent enough about gardening. I wasn't even diligent about the notes I kept on gardening. I meant for them to be a source for a book I'd write about city life, rural life, ecology, and plants, including weeding and gardening—in fact, I had intended to be quaintly philosophical about nearly everything. I didn't and wasn't.

I grew tired of facing my shortcomings. When I started gardening those years ago, I read gardening books and thumbed gardening encyclopedias. I learned reasonably well what one *ought* to do in soil preparation, fertilization, aeration, irrigation, crop location, and plant preparation, but I mostly did it all scattershot. I sometimes got sidetracked reading about plants and where they came from and how they got their names and spent more

time with that than I did getting the seeds in the ground by the right phase of the moon.

I kept remembering the words of an old song, and would find myself singing it as I weeded down the rows:

> You may keep your nerve through June and July,
> But along comes August with that same clear sky.
> Then sinners will pray, and saints will complain—
> They'll cry, "O Lord, won't you send us some rain?"

One morning I went out to the garden early and saw tiny shoots just breaking the ground. Early the next morning, I looked again, and the little shoots had already burned. My notes for the previous day showed a temperature of 110.

I got to thinking about Grandpa Durham, my mother's father. In 1919 he was farming in Denton County, not far from here. My mother still remembers the day vividly. He went into the cotton field to hoe. They saw him stop and bend and look, then move a little and stop and bend and look, then move across the field and stop and bend and look. He picked up his hoe and came to the house without looking back.

"Let's pack," he said. "We're going to West Texas." He didn't say more. Later they learned that boll weevils had taken his cotton, and the crop was gone.

When I saw the little shoots burned, I kept thinking of Grandpa Durham. Then, since my mother was not in hearing range, I said, "The hell with it," went in the house, and sat down with a cup of coffee.

Maybe Grandpa Durham would have understood.

A Little Evidence That the World Exists:
Some Features of a Landscape

I

I remember a late norther. I remember watching a robin sitting on the windowsill. He was coveting the sun, hunting a little warmth, looking as if he'd had a second thought about coming this far so soon. He scrunched down in his feathers and turned tail into a wind that whipped and chilled and gusted way more than he and I thought appropriate.

2

One March, I remember, robins claimed the school ground where I passed, mornings, on my short way round to work.

Something they found in the grass exacted more time than I was worth. They walked and picked before me, around me, undismayed. I wove and waded among them. No bird startled at my feet into flight.

I wouldn't have wished it otherwise. I didn't want to bother them at feed across the school ground.

I don't know what is everlasting—not birds, I'd guess, surely not these. Still, on a March morning, I took great pleasure, finding that some of the things of earth were undisturbed about my passing.

3

My office window that time let me see a shaded walk, a cornice, a cornerstone in the next building, and especially a tall oak tree higher than the hall it shades. In fall it goes to orange and buff and ochre and takes its shape against the farther tree that holds a dusty, browning green longer. I've tried to learn why the farther tree holds green a little longer, have asked and had diverse answers, all true, I suppose, and wrong.

Once, I remember, two helicopters hurried down my window beyond the high branches of the oak tree. My son says they're keen, and I know they're marvels: I've seen them bumblebee in

bands, back and turn; I expect they could dance a schottische
or quadrille.

Still, I was glad for the quiet when they were gone. The cornerstone yonder was still there, and the tree, although its leaves
were falling. I resolved that, when it was time next fall, and a
norther weaves the color trunkward, I would name the leaves,
and wait, and watch them quietly as they fall.

4

Another March. March 5, some year. I saw a mockingbird sitting on the street sign where I turn. He was whistling winter gone
from the thirty-one hundred block of Odessa Street. I assumed
that the word would get around: mockingbirds speak to cardinals.

5

Another March. March 10, 1976. Outside my office window,
in the near magnolia tree's top, a robin spent the first half of the
day arranging the world for spring. Rostrum-raised, she (or he,
as the case may be) pulpit-voiced plans: instructions here, directions there, chore assignments yonder.

I was unable, at the moment, to share her fullest hopes (or
his, as the case may be), but wished her luck (or him).

I reckoned, after all, that the day just might be the day it all
takes shape. She just might get things disposed (or he, as the case
may be). I knew I'd be glad to join right in if she (or he) should
manage to order us all for a season.

6

The order I make of things is, they tell me, usually a little
wrong. I take wherever I stand to be the Great Divide, and as-
sume that West, open country, begins just to my right, wherever
I happen to be. Then it's always my world, however I happen to
see it.

But once in a while, I get a little evidence that the world exists, and maybe I don't.

I remember, for example, the bed on the screened-in porch at

Grandpa's house. I came only later to know that it was ill-kept and none too clean, but it was mine in the dark and moon those times I stayed a while in summers. I could be sure of corn on the cob, fresh from the field, to eat just about every day. My grandmother didn't seem to mind if I went for the record in eating ears of corn, and I was glad enough to try for it. I could be sure of time, time for walking and looking and sitting and chunking rocks. I could be sure of checker games and domino games and time.

We went to bed early, soon after dark. Grandpa was tired, there were few books, and coal oil for the lamps was never cheap.

The screened-in porch was blue, and the bed and porch were mine and all the world outside, and the swing at the other end

of the porch. It creaked its music past my yearning, an old, young, dear, sad tune to hold their folk and days, my hope, all loss I knew would come. The windmill down the way was mine, its music creaking too, its tune uncanny and impossible. It played old time, small hope, the melody of loss.

I could not always find myself, but I knew the world was there: five ears of corn to eat if I should choose at one great feast and checkers and dominoes and time and house and porch and dark and swing and down the way the windmill song. Not I, but the world was there, all around.

They died, those two, before I knew their lives. The house burned down and bed and swing. The windmill fell to ruin. The field of corn turned brown and bare.

The world was there, well evidenced, and I was not, was waiting to be found, was not, but oh, I heard sweet music once.

Some Things Change, and Some Things Don't

Early in the fall semester I went away for Uncle Martin's funeral. I don't think anyone missed me—I left after my last class on Monday and was back for my first class on Wednesday, and I had no Tuesday class.

I went with my father and my brother and Uncle Dee, my father's brother. The funeral service was in Jayton, a little town of about 750 souls, though there are still those who say you shouldn't count Boone Bilberry. Jayton lies something like 225 miles almost straight west of Fort Worth, but is otherwise not very close to anyplace that outsiders would know. I suppose Uncle Martin wasn't really my uncle. He was my Aunt Mary's husband, but I knew him as my uncle and that made it so when I was young. It was still so when I went with the others to his funeral. That hadn't changed.

Uncle Martin and Aunt Mary had lived for years in New Mexico. They left Jayton almost as soon as my family did. It was about 1939 or 1940, and I don't think there was more than $27.60 among all of the citizens of the town. They just kept paying each other parts of the $27.60 for various goods and services, and the money kept changing hands, but didn't increase. In New Mexico he eventually became a successful business contractor.

I didn't see my Uncle Martin and Aunt Mary for years after we all left Jayton, and I suppose I saw them only two or three times briefly in all the forty and more years after Jayton. When they opened the casket at the brief service beside the grave — as Baptists and others sometimes do — I looked at Uncle Martin, and he was a whole lot smaller than he should have been. He was big and strong when I was a boy, but now he was small. That had changed.

The proper church funeral service had already been held in New Mexico, where Uncle Martin and Aunt Mary lived. But Jayton was still home, and so they brought his body there for burial. While we were at the cemetery waiting for the service to start, we talked quietly in bunches, as people do. My brother and I wandered a little away from the others. From the cemetery, you can see all of Jayton, and we had noticed that Jayton was greener than it was when we lived there. Trees that didn't exist when we knew Jayton had been planted, and they had grown, and the town was green in the distance. My brother and I remembered only browns and grays and dirty yellows and sandy reds from the Jayton we knew in the Dust Bowl years. That had changed.

When I knew Uncle Martin those days in Jayton, he was the nearest thing the town had to a general handyman and builder. He would dig cisterns and septic tanks, patch roofs, put stucco on houses, and do whatever people had to do that they couldn't do themselves. Then they'd pay him part of the town's $27.60, and he would go and pay somebody else for something he needed or some debt he owed. In the summers, I sometimes tagged along after him, riding in the back of his old pickup and fetching tools to him. He didn't pay much attention to me, and I didn't pay much attention to him. We were just there. When the mill didn't run, my father sometimes worked with Uncle Martin. The mill ran so long as there was a cotton crop, and the better the cotton crop, the longer the mill ran. Sometimes it didn't run very long, and my father worked with Uncle Martin. I remember the two of them, one mixing cement, the other pouring and smoothing it, and I remember that it was good to watch the rhythm they created together and the muscles playing along their backs and down

their arms, and the steady way they had of working that would let them get through a whole day of hard work in a hot sun. My memories of that, and the fact of it, haven't changed.

But somewhere along the way Uncle Martin got to be smaller than I thought, and Aunt Mary got to be older than I thought.

We all met at the Baptist Church (the new one, now twenty years old, not the old one that I remembered), and went together to the cemetery. The cemetery lies maybe three-quarters of a mile past the last house on the northwest edge of town. There were maybe forty of us, mostly distant relatives that I didn't know. When we got to the cemetery, there was the quiet talking, and then we stood in a half-circle around the grave. There were chairs for Aunt Mary and a few others. That was when they opened the casket, so those who wanted to could see Uncle Martin. The service was short. People stood and visited, and some said goodbyes, thinking they might not see each other again. That was as I remembered it from old days at funerals. That hadn't changed.

Those who remained went back to the church to visit and wait for the lunch that the women of the church were providing. I had

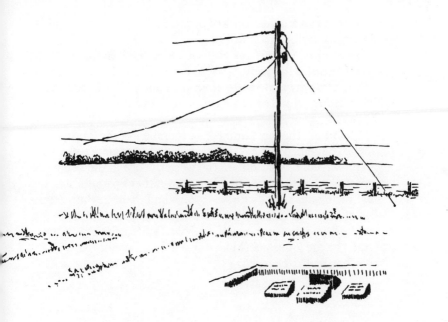

an hour, so I walked to the house I remember best. It's the last house on the north edge of town. It's used now for storing hay, but it had the shape and the lie on the land that I remembered.

Scarcely ten yards beyond the house the canyons began. There were a lot more mesquite trees than I remembered, so I couldn't see as far as before.

But the canyons were as deep and rough as I remembered. They hadn't changed, and maybe someday I could still have them with all the time I needed.

I walked back to the church and visited for a while with the pleasant and energetic young minister. I asked him to explain a mystery for me, something I had always wondered about: How did the women of a church know that it was time to prepare food and to take care of families at times like funerals, when most or all of the people had come from out of town. He smiled and said, "They just know." That hadn't changed.

He was pleased that his congregation had grown from an average Sunday attendance of 70 the year before to an average of 110 during the current year. I asked him if most of the congregation came from Jayton itself or if a good many came in from farms in the country. He said the majority were from Jayton, but that several families did come in from the north half of the county. I asked him why none came from the south half of the county. He smiled again and said, "There's no one out there." That hadn't changed.

After lunch the most immediate members of the family went back to the cemetery for just a few minutes. The grave was closed and mounded. Not far off, on the western edge of the cemetery, were the graves of my grandparents, my father's parents, and the grave of an aunt I hardly knew. If you stand there, at the western edge of the cemetery, and look west, you can just about see forever. In 1938, when my grandfather was buried there, I thought it must be the lonesomest place on earth. I thought that in 1983, too. That hadn't changed.

Come Fall

Any season, I know, can be melancholy, for all seasons send us down toward death. Fall is woeful enough for me, though there's reason to think otherwise.

I have often looked forward to fall and the beginning of the school year with high expectations. When I was young, there were many reasons for such keen longings. One was the arrival of the Sears Roebuck catalog, which — in 1937, for example — offered almost inexhaustible pleasures. Waiting for it was a delicious excitement. I never knew how it happened — perhaps there was a reverberation in the air — but everyone seemed to know when the catalogs arrived at the post office. When she thought I was old enough, my mother would send me to the little rock post office just off the square to get our catalog. Then I would start home thinking maybe I would tear the wrapping off and stop to look at it along the way. I never did that. I think now that the ritual of getting the catalog home was too significant for me to violate it. I didn't think that then. I just got home as fast as I could. Then

I could take the admiring first look, flipping through the pages just to see the pictures before I settled down for slow, dreamy looking and reading. There seemed no end to its uses. My mother would study the book and send in the yearly order, and a yearly box would come with the year's clothes, and every year she'd somehow manage to get our Christmas presents out of the box without our knowing they were there. Reading lessons were to be had from the catalog, and instruction in fantasy. If you were to be an expert fantasist in 1937, you didn't stop with adopting a particular cowboy identity; you imaged out that identity with clothes of a particular cut and color, and with a very particular hat and a certain gun belt, displayed in the toy section. Models for drawing were also available in the catalog, and since we lived in a rural area, it also had its final uses. Indeed, that's one of the reasons we chose Sears Roebuck over Montgomery Ward, for the quality of the paper.

But I'm not young anymore. The catalog doesn't come anymore. Even fall doesn't come in the same way anymore. When I look back now, I think that there was scarcely ever a time when those high expectations of fall were entirely free from a certain sadness. I wouldn't have known to say that then. But I do remember standing on the rim of the canyons, late afternoons, looking as far as I could see and being suddenly lonesome—for what, I couldn't have said at the time, but now I think I was already lonesome for all that I would lose, for all that I would never gain, for all that I would never say, see, hear, or be.

Still, there have always been reasons for thinking fall a happy season. It offers a rest from the heat and drought that are ours in the summer here on the edge of the Great American Desert. It brings the new year. I've been in school one way or another for forty-nine years. When that is the circumstance, you come to know that January 1 is just a holiday. The new year actually commences sometime after September 1. Things begin then. Things left off for the summer are picked up again. If you are a schoolteacher, as I am, you even get to believe that the first day of school is Resurrection Day, and this time around you'll do better. Sometimes that feeling lasts awhile. Sometimes it doesn't. When fall comes and the time is right, there is a moon beyond magic to see. They say that when the harvest moon is full and you see it large and low in the east—if you're not surrounded by all the things we've built to block our vision—they say, I was about to mention, that you can restore the moon to its proper proportion by turning your back on it and then bending over to look at it between your legs. I never tried that. I don't know why anyone would want to.

Fall is turning time for more than schoolteachers. Out in the first stretches of the great lonesome where I grew part way, farmers probably knew in their bones what harvest time would bring long before the fall came. And yet, and yet, I remember, when picking time drew near—out there, that's September and early October for cotton—there'd be a hush until the cotton was in and we learned what kind of year we'd have. Since there were prizes to be given to the man who brought in the first bale of cotton, some would hurry picking time back into August and maybe use up the first slim harvest of thirty acres just to get that first bale in. Mostly, though, people waited for picking time.

Waiting for fall, I know, can be good. When fall comes, it can, I know, be the best season.

I remember a Tuesday not long ago (it was September 25, 1984, and my birthday) when a cold front came in and dropped the temperature here appreciably. It wasn't much as cold fronts go, but it was pleasant. On Wednesday I mentioned the term "blue norther" in my freshman class. I wanted to find out who knew the term, and I wanted to find out whether or not students from other parts of the country had names for particular weather events in their territory. Most did not know the term "blue norther," those who had heard it couldn't tell much about it, and the search for special names in other parts of the country didn't turn up much. I dropped the matter as not much of a cause and a lost one anyway.

Then, later that same day, I discovered that the local paper (the *Fort Worth Star Telegram*) had a front-page feature about "blue northers." the article began with a tall tale:

> Shoot. This isn't cold. Bob Murphy of Nacogdoches remembers the time a Blue Norther went through East Texas.
>
> "A woman set a pot of boiling water out on the back porch," he said. "She was going to wash, you know. It froze so fast that the ice was still hot."

What happened that Tuesday wasn't a blue norther. It was just a fast-moving front that dropped the official temperature from a high of 90° at 1 P.M. to 61° by 3 P.M. That's close, but not a blue norther.

Blue northers are common in Texas, Oklahoma, and Kansas and can be felt much farther. They are scarcely worth mentioning, I guess, *sub specie aeternitatis*, and other winds have names as well known or better. The chinook, for example, is a warm, dry wind that blows off the eastern slopes of the Rocky Mountains in the northwestern part of this country and in western Canada. There's a dry, sandy wind off the west coast of Africa that blows from the interior. It's called *harmattan*. Central and southern Mediterranean areas are subject to very warm southerly winds that bring air from the hot desert interior of northern Africa. These winds, the *Britannica* says, "are abnormally dry and hazy and are most prominent in the spring when cyclonic winds are common and the sea is much cooler than the desert. They bring oppressive weather and often damage to vegetation." The general name for these winds is sirocco, but people in particular areas have given them their own special names. In Malta and Egypt, they are known as *khamsin*. They are called *simoon* in northeast Africa and Arabia. In parts of northern Africa they are called *leste*, and in southeast Spain they are called *leveche*. I guess the blue norther may be a cousin to the mistral, which is a cold northerly wind that comes down out of Europe and breaks through the barrier formed by the Alps and the Pyrenees into Italy and the Mediterranean.

I don't know any of these winds in a personal sort of way, but I am acquainted with the blue norther. To me, on the small side of eternity, the blue norther is maybe the most exhilarating event it's possible to know. On the day a blue norther comes, the wind will be blowing maybe pretty gently, most likely from the south or southwest. Then, when you're not paying attention, the wind will stop, and the air will be still except for an occasional twist that will swirl the leaves for a moment. If you have been paying attention, you will have seen by this time in the north and northwest a blue line of clouds. If you are familiar with blue northers, that time of stillness is high with expectation. Then, bye and bye, it comes, sometimes with rain or sleet, often dry because it whistles in and through so fast it doesn't have time to rain. It will take your breath for a moment if it's a good one, on some occasions dropping the temperature fifty degrees in an afternoon. If you're out in the open when the norther strikes, and if you face into it and give yourself to it, for a moment or two you'll get a quick glimpse of a notion about what it feels like to be the Lord God Almighty riding the wind down along the slope of the Rockies, across the Panhandle, down off the Caprock, and home.

That ought to be enough to make fall a sweet time. It isn't. I'm not young anymore. I seldom go out and give myself to northers anymore. The catalog doesn't come anymore. The harvest is past, the summer is ended, and I am not saved.

I have waited on the promises of picking time and have once in a while seen the fulfillment of promises. But even when I was young and stood on the rim of the canyons looking into the blue distance, an autumnal chill sometimes shivered my bones and wrapped around me like a winding sheet. Since, even in happy Septembers and radiant Octobers, that autumnal chill has cut deeper and deeper. Somewhere along the way I learned to expect grief. I will be sad come fall, and I think there's scant hope for consolation. If fall can be a sweet, high time, fresh with new beginnings, it is also a leaving time, a parting time, a dying time.

Sometimes, I think, small things whirl around in our heads and become momentous. Whirligigs become monsters, and interruptions of habit become signs of general disorder. For most of the last forty-nine years, I mentioned a while ago, fall began when the school year began, and the year began when fall came. For most of those years, that time was terminus and inception, and I set my tempo to that calendar. We'd wind summer down, get past Labor Day, wait for a skittering whisper of wind out of the northwest, start school, and it would be fall and a new year. Then, a few years ago, the world changed my schedule. The beginning of school—usually along between September 10 and September 20—had more significance, I've already said, than New Year's Day in the old time. But they are out there; the they as in "they say," decided to start school earlier. Now we begin while it's still high, hot summer, perhaps as early as August 20. I've lost the fall, my tempo, my starting time for the year.

On reflection, this little change becomes in my mind a sign

of a general whomper-jawedness that I suffer from. Perhaps many of us suffer so. Though the fellow in the White House leads cheers and tells us that everything will be all right if we just wave the flag, pray in school, and learn to be rich, signs of whomper-jawedness do persist. Change waits in momentous rushes, so fast that we cannot hope to keep pace. If that is not the actuality, it seems to be, with overwhelming immediacy. We look about us and see a nature that is always under threat of destruction, a past that is torn up, plowed under, and cemented over directly behind us. We know a famine is yet to come. We experience abusive tempos and lacerating doubts. The maxims, wisdom, folk knowledge of our nurturing are repudiated. The language is assaulted. We see and hear a new literacy that isn't too literate. Sometimes thoughtlessness allows us a few months of euphoria; more often, with Scarlett, we get a little ease by postponing thought. But waiting, there is a burden we'll not escape, a burden, as Norman Cousins put it a while ago, of imminent, self-inflicted defeat, of imperfect human organizations, of onrushing depersonalization, of dread, the dread of final loneliness. We're sometimes afraid that it's all going away, as we dread that we are dying, as we always are. I know that not everyone is as cowardly as I, as timorous and fearful, as accustomed to expecting grief as I. But surely somewhere out there sits someone who lives as I do, waiting, like the Comanches in Palo Duro Canyon. To be sure, they had gone to the Red River to join the Kiowas and to follow Ishatai in a last great Sun Dance to nerve themselves up, as we sometimes do, but then, not much later, they found themselves in Palo Duro Canyon, waiting, and when they looked up, the future came down upon them, down the sides of the canyon with Mackenzie's troopers. Then the world was over for the Comanches, though none died on the spot. The *People* were done. They found the ultimate loneliness that we sit and wait for.

Against the loneliness I have no stay. Against the loneliness I have stored no treasures. I have only quick images to cheer me and dear, though pale, memories. I haven't held on to history, or got history told right to linger over. I have made no films, kept no scrapbook, and such photographs as we have are scattered in a hundred places. I can't get the sweet past to stay with me. Not long after he died, my grandfather's house burned. Detritus and midden shards alone remain of the past. When fall comes, times slip away; when the season turns, I am sad despite myself, sad even when I am surrounded by riches. I have told myself, time and again, to mark each day, to note it, to hold it, and to celebrate it in memory, but the season turns, and everything changes, and I live with regrets that, if small, are deep to me. Living in the midst of regrets, small or large, is hell enough, I think. I'd not want to be misunderstood, or to see in myself what is not there. Somberness is not my constant garb, and I do not regularly achieve such profundity as would consign me to hell or any other location. Mostly, I dawdle time away; mostly, I am about as trivial in thought and deed as the next fellow. But when fall comes and the fallen leaves skitter before a twist of wind, I'll be sad.

When summer is still to come, I always expect to finish out the chores I've set myself, get beyond them, and go on to grand chores not yet imagined. Once in a while I manage to finish something or other. One summer my son and I built a storage shed out back. My two daughters put their palms into the wet cement base and marked the date. We built it square and neat, roofed it well, and spaced good cedar shingles for its final wall coating. We painted the trim properly, which is to say that I was not allowed to hold the paintbrush. I sometimes see things as they really should look, but my style is a quick slap of paint and off to rest. One summer I cleaned the garage despite my friend who stopped by, looked at the mess, and allowed as how that one summer wouldn't cover the job.

If it seems that summer passes with little done, I'd grant the judgment, but you have to allow for the weeks I spend before each chore in planning keen craftsmanship. But then I always turn out to be a jackleg carpenter, and the objects of my crafting range only from tolerable to half-assed.

One summer we made a patio down the north stretch between the fence and the house, alongside kitchen and porch.

The storage shed still stands square, the cedar shingles gone grey and silver. The garage is still mostly clean. The patio is there, a jigsaw puzzle of heavy cedar boards outlining the shapes of cement. Enough, I guess, and foolish to hope that carving and sawing and mixing and smoothing would somehow stop time's running.

When I was ready to make the patio and had laid in all the material I'd need, my father came to get me started and especially to show me how to mix the cement. I watched the swing of the deep-bellied shovel, easy and economical, up to the mixer. Mud, he calls it, the cement he makes, and tilts the mix into my wheelbarrow. He makes a batch, I tote and pour, and we smooth it out together. The mud he makes is good, though there is no recipe. I judge his bones know in the sweep of the deep-bellied shovel when it's good cement, and he tells me just to look, and when it looks about right, then it will be cement. My son and I made the last batches. Their color and texture are not to his standard, but he remarks that the patio probably won't crack before I do.

I puzzle and twist to find out why in the midst of good I find sorrow. Sharp images remain from those summers of making and cleaning and building—David stopping and stretching out on the ground, to supervise my work, he says; Cathy in overalls yearning to touch the little wild kitten who eventually came to captivate the household; Mindy filling the plastic water pool she'd played in before, notifying all concerned that she was not filling the little pool to play in it as in summers before when she was little, but that this summer she'd use it for sunbathing; my wife guarding the paintbrush; my father, mixed in that stretch of cement beside the house, caught, too, in my arm's remembrance of the steady swing of the shovel I learned first from him, mixing mud those hot summer days. Such images flicker and pass, flicker and stay until, instead of finding joy, I must shake my shoulders to keep from crying for such sweet times passing.

Things change. Everything changes. Nothing holds still. Houses burn. People leave. People die. Disorder surrounds me, and I can't hold on to anything long enough to show how dear it was to me. The past disappears out from under me, and one day it will catch me and I will disappear, too. I have waited for grief, and never knew that when it came, it would look very much like myself. I will be sad come fall, and do not expect consolation. The harvest is past, the summer is ended, and I am not saved.

Lost in West Texas: A Little Travelogue, There and Elsewhere

M y young friend told me not long ago that when I talk about West Texas, I'm talking about New Jersey. She and her husband, that other young friend, came to Texas two years ago from Perth Amboy, by way of Providence, Rhode Island, much filled with news from Perth Amboy, and great love. I hope what she said is so.

I was in New Jersey once for three days, and no more since. With hundreds of others, and like thousands of others before us, I came back from Germany on a troop ship in 1952. I study the map now, trying to learn where I was and what I saw, but I can't make it out. From my chancy recollection, I'd guess we docked in Jersey City. We went straight to a train that took us directly to Camp Kilmer, where during three days we were poked on and prodded a little, and then were separated into smaller groups to be sent variously homeward. Camp Kilmer later for a little while became Fort Kilmer, but I can't find it on my map, and my young friends tell me that a community college stands on the ground that Camp Kilmer once occupied. They show me where it is, but

I can't find any place along that route from docking somewhere to a train ride to Camp Kilmer that I can remember. I was there, but I wasn't there. It's gone from me, and I am gone.

Other people seem to know territories in which I was lost, or never found. My young friends point to a spot on the map almost directly west of Perth Amboy, out Industrial Highway, where Camp Kilmer once stood. I remember that friends from my platoon, far more adventurous than I, took the opportunity of pass time in those three days at Camp Kilmer to go into Manhattan. When I look at the map, it seems a long way, and mysterious, but they apparently knew how to be in a place better than I did.

Sometimes I think that everyone knows that better than I do. I can't find the land. I can't get found in the land.

I told my other young friend, my young friend's husband, that I can't get everything filed and sorted so that I can retrieve it. He told me that pretty soon a machine will come to solve my problem. Then, he says, if I fragment everything, file it, and index it all, I'll be able to call up any part of everything, or the whole. I know that's true so far as the piles of papers strewn around my desk are concerned, but I doubt it works with what I only half-remember, half-know.

There, where I only half-remember and half-know, I can't get things sorted out. What is the difference between what occurred out there in West Texas and what I think occurred? What is the difference between what I think occurred and what I never heard of? What is the difference between the way it looked out there and the way it was reported? What is the difference between the way it looked out there and the way I believe or dream or remember it looked? Even when I go to look for myself, I cannot tell. Is there someone who can tell me what really happened, what it really looked like? Can I get a witness?

I am lost from the country, can't find myself there or here, and the country is lost to me. I have no scrapbook but the fragments in my mind, though I do cherish a few photographs I made around Jayton and Spur and the Croton Breaks. While I have never learned to believe in photographs, I have fingered two in particular so much that they are bent and wrinkled. One shows the little house on the Lowrance ranch. It sat right on the rim between the edge of Jayton and the first canyon in the Breaks. We lived there when

I was in the second grade, but when I made the picture it was being used for hay storage. Sometime within the last three years, they took it down, or maybe it fell down. I look at the picture, but I can't find the house, or myself in it. The other was taken from the highway a few miles outside of Spur, looking up under the trestle to the rise and my grandfather's farmhouse. Trestle and house are gone now, and when I look at the picture, I can't find all of us there, or see just what the place was like those times.

Sometimes I think it's all lost, irretrievably gone. *Nostalgia* takes it origin from the Greek *nostos*, or "return home," and *algia*, or "pain." I understand that it is more than a general ache, but I don't know the home I long to recapture. *Topophilia*, or love of place, seems entirely understandable to me; indeed, I find myself nostalgic for places that never were my home, and I can't find them, either.

I have not seen the great synagogue in Vilnius, in Lithuania, and never will, and cannot find Lithuania. The first stones of the synagogue, they say, were laid in 1571, but after all this time I have not seen them, and never will. The building was a ruin when World War II ended. The Soviets tore it down and made the Jewish cemetery into an athletic field. They play across the graves.

And how did it look, I wonder, when Riga fell, and how can I find Latvia? How can I learn to see what the lady I knew saw when Riga fell? When she walked across Europe? How was she situated with the sun, and what did she see across those miles, miles, from Riga to Poland, across Poland to Germany, across Germany to France, at last to Paris, at last to Austin, Texas? How was she situated with the sun, and what did she see? I'm waiting to know.

I haven't walked, as I have thought to walk, and look, and look, from Fort Worth to Weatherford to Mineral Wells, past the Brazos to Breckenridge to Albany to Leuders to Stamford to Old Glory to Aspermont to Swenson to Jayton.

Grandma and Grandpa Durham died in Spur, or near. Their graves are side by side in the Spur cemetery, one stone to mark them both. Far to one side of the cemetery is a marker for two of Mackenzie's troopers, who died of an excess of Comanche arrows not far away. Near the far edge of the cemetery is the grave of a little boy, dead at six in 1935. The marker on his grave was roughly shaped of poor cement. His marbles are embedded in it. How, I wonder, did the Durhams look when they were married, and what did they see when they first looked across those fields? What did the troopers find along Duck Creek? Did their feet determine the creek bottom I was to wade? How did the little boy bend to shoot his taw? I have not yet seen them, though I have looked.

Nor have I seen the dome and star atop the Moscow synagogue on Arkhipova Street. The building grew in the 1880s, to be topped by the great dome and star. When it was completed, the bureaucrats ordered dome and star taken down. Too high above the other buildings, they said; some identities must not be quite so visible.

And I have not yet taken my father down the Mississippi on a steamboat. We'd look and look and ease on down past Hannibal, Cairo, Memphis, on down. It's too late now; my time has grown short, and his is shorter.

I have not seen the fourteenth-century synagogue in Worms.

After 1945, it became a memorial for congregations that no longer exist. Row on row, they are not there, and I have not found them.

I read the labels on the cans and jars along the shelves of the delicatessen and wonder how things are in Bucharest and Odessa.

My other grandparents lie side by side at the western edge of the cemetery in Jayton. Graves outnumber extant citizens. The western edge of the cemetery in Jayton is the lonesomest place on earth. If you stand there looking west, you can see forever, but not all. I have looked, but only by quick moments, else it's too much, and never enough.

I can't find Jayton. I go looking, looking. I go looking to find faces and ways and places, but map and memory fail, and what I have is all there is, my little memory text.

And I am lost. I always find myself trying to think through West Texas, out of West Texas, back into West Texas. Scarcely any work proceeds long without angling somehow through, into, or out of West Texas. I'm always looking for West Texas or my part of it, and not finding it. My part of West Texas doesn't show up much in books. Can I get a witness? Why is it never there? Can I get a witness?

Sometimes I imagine that if I could just get situated right with the sun and look just so, I could see it as it looked to all those others, and know what it was like. Probably not, but I need a witness.

Some come close.

Some come close, but they don't tell me what I want to hear, don't show me what I want to see, don't validate my memory.

Interwoven is close, though a little too east, and about another breed of folk.

Max Crawford's *Lords of the Plains* is almost there, maybe there and I don't recognize it.

Some come close, and tell me episodes.

Harold B. Simpson's *Cry Comanche: The 2nd U.S. Cavalry in Texas, 1855–1861*, tells a story of Major George H. Thomas, his troopers, and a certain Comanche that I often come back to. The story ends near the Double Mountains in 1859:

On the morning of August 25 Thomas' Delaware guide, Doss, came across an Indian trail about 25 miles east of Mountain Pass, in present Taylor County. The wagons were immediately sent to Camp Cooper, and the command with pack mules started in pursuit in a northwest direction, marching 40 miles before nightfall. Thomas continued the pursuit at daylight on the 26th and at 7 A.M. Doss discovered a band of 13 Indians, breaking camp on the Salt Fork of the Brazos, about a mile and a half away. Thomas, as soon as he received the scout's report, started his command at a gallop and arrived at the Indian encampment a few minutes after the Indians had left. Now a running battle took place with the Indians having a half mile lead. For over three miles the pursuit continued, the soldiers following the Indians so closely that they abandoned their loose horses. As the chase continued one warrior, "an old Comanche," dropped off his horse and armed with only a bow and arrows and a lance defied the pursuers. In their eagerness to dispatch the lone Indian the cavalrymen (and bandsmen) pressed too closely, and consequently several of his arrows and lance thrusts took effect. Major Thomas was hit in both the chin and chest by arrows, but a thick beard and stout chin and heavy hair on his barrel chest fortunately turned both barbs, although leaving painful cuts. The venerable Comanche before he fell managed to wound Privates William Murphy and Hugh Clark of Company D, Chief Bugler August Hausser and bandsmen John Zito and Casper Siddel. Murphy, who later died of his wounds, Zito and Siddel were all struck by arrows, as was Thomas. Clark and Hausser were wounded by weak lance thrusts administered by the warrior after he had been shot "twenty or more" times. No greater example of self-sacrifice is recorded in the annals of Indian warfare on the western frontier.

Thomas was of the opinion that had their pursuit not been stopped by the old warrior, his command could have caught and brought to justice the 12 other fleeing Comanches. (pp. 151–52)

The opening four chapters of W. C. Holden's *The Espuela Land and Cattle Company* tell me far more than I knew about the lay of the land from the Caprock eastward into Dickens County, and about the natural flora and fauna. I learn there, too, that Mackenzie's trail crossed the site of the old Spur Inn (it burned in 1940) on the way to campsites on Duck Creek, not far from Soldiers Mound.

In an earlier paper ("The Problem of Stealing on the Spur Ranch," *West Texas Historical Association Year Book*, June, 1932, pp. 25–42), Holden quotes an 1889 letter from Spur Ranch manager S. W. Lomax, fretful of "the cattle stealing and brand burning that is, and has for some time, been going on to the south of us between Salt Fork and Double Mountain River in Kent and Scurry Counties." Holden also tells of an "exciting bit of robbery" that took place on the Spur Ranch in February, 1889:

> Two "bad men" with considerable reputation entered the company store one cold night while Dick Ware, the store keeper, and a ranch hand named Sowell were dozing by the fire, and proceeded to stage an unusual type of robbery, although not the kind one reads about in western fiction. They tied and blind-folded Ware and Sowell and leisurely began to help themselves to what they wanted in the store. They took money, clothing, boots, ammunition, candy, groceries, stamps and newspapers from the post office, and some cheap novels. Loaded with all the merchandise they could conveniently carry they left in a southwesterly direction, taking with them several of the company horses. The next day a posse made up of a deputy sheriff from Estacado, Crosby County, and several of the cowboys from the ranch started in pursuit. The desperados' weakness for literature proved their undoing. While they were resting under some trees in Yellowhouse Canyon, calmly reading the dime novels, the posse overtook and quietly surrounded them. So absorbed were they in the stories, that an array of six shooter and Winchester barrels were pointing at them from every direction before they were aware of any intrusion. (pp. 28–29)

In the ensuing trial at Estacado, a letter from Fred Horsbrugh (Lomax's successor as manager of the Spur Ranch) remarks that "the courthouse was new, and so were the lawyers, and such an opportunity to hear their own voices in the new room was a sudden streak of luck to them." When the case was over, Horsbrugh reports, "the lawyers got to fighting fists-to-cuff, and in the confusion in the court, one of the prisoners tried to escape and was shot down in the room a yard or two from where I stood" (p. 30).

How Grandpa Durham came to have his farm acres just east of the Spur Ranch, or maybe inside the ranch territory, I do not know. J. E. Ericson tells a little, but not about Grandpa (in "Colonization of the Spur Farm Lands," *West Texas Historical Association Year Book*, October, 1955, pp. 41–53). The Spur Ranch began in 1883, and was sold to the Espuela Land and Cattle Company, Limited, of London, in 1885. By 1907, Ericson reports, the "land holdings had been increased to 439,972 acres, located in Dickens,

Kent, Garza, and Crosby Counties" (p. 41). By March, 1908, the ranch had been sold to S. M. Swenson and Sons for $1,400,000.

On November 11, 1909, after having helped to finance and direct the Stamford and Northwestern Railroad [later the Wichita Valley Line of the Burlington Railroad] to the present location of the City of Spur, the Swensons and their associates placed on sale the town lots in that city and the surrounding farm lands. On that date the only structures within the townsite were the Western Hotel, the townsite land office, the depot, the section houses for the railroad, and the office of *The Texas Spur*, a weekly newspaper.

Thirty days later, the new town boasted a population of over 700 people, with fifty business houses, over sixty residences, a telephone system, temporary water works, a public school, and a railroad terminal. At the end of three months there were over 300 residences and more than seventy business houses. (p. 41)

As Ericson reports, the opening of the Spur farm lands, probably more than any other single factor, helped to account for an increase in the aggregate population of Dickens, Kent, Garza, and Crosby counties from 3,023 in 1900 to 27,321 in 1930. But Ericson doesn't tell about Grandpa Durham.

I know that he was farming near Denton in 1918. When the boll weevils took his crop, he moved the family by wagon to West Texas. I know that he sharecropped for a while in the Centerview community between Jayton and Swenson, but I don't know all that he did between 1918 and about 1935, when I began to know him. I do know that one of the promotional booklets issued for the Spur Farm Lands, sometime after 1919, told prospective buyers this:

To the man who wishes to engage in straight farming, we offer high-class farm lands, suited to a great variety of farm crops. . . .
Cotton, in addition to the feed crops . . . is reliably grown here. There is no boll weevil. (Ericson, p. 51)

Some come close, but they do not tell me what I want to hear, do not show me what I want to see.

In *The Big Ranch Country*, J. W. Williams tells a little more, tells about driving from Aspermont to Jayton, seeing the Double Mountains some ten miles south in plain relief, tells how the "two great mounds that can be seen for forty miles in some directions have been a landmark to travelers since the days of the California Gold Rush" (p. 52), tells about O. J. Wiren and the Two Circle Bar Ranch:

By 1886 some 30,000 cows, perhaps, proudly wore his Two Circle Bar brand on an immense range of some 500 or more square miles of grass. So great was his dominion that sunrise caught some of his herds nipping grass in the shade of the Double Mountains in Stonewall County while sunset found others grazing contentedly far over in Kent County, a full day's buggy ride to the west. Some of his cows sipped the putrid waters of Croton Creek several miles to the north of present Jayton, while others found their liquid refreshments in small water holes on the south slope of the Double Mountain River thirty miles away. (p. 53)

Williams also tells about driving, farther to the north, from Guthrie to Dickens:

On this return to Dickens . . . I looked southward toward the Croton Breaks. This chopped-up patch on the map of West Texas, not very plainly visible from my road, undoubtedly would take first prize among the bad lands of South Plains.
In one rather ludicrous particular it out-does Bryce's Canyon which a modern magazine writer describes as "one hell of a place to lose a cow." The Croton Breaks, though picturesque in their own right, cannot compare from a scenic viewpoint with magnificent Bryce's Canyon, but they are even a worse place to lose a cow. The Matadors carefully rounded up their cattle from these bad lands in 1936. Some 600 head were driven from the fluted piece of earth. Among them were many six-year-old bulls and cows that had never seen a branding iron—Mavericks in the original sense of the word! But even more unbelievable than these curiosities of the modern day, there were at least 100 steers that had long run wild like animals in the jungle. Some of them bore an old Matador date brand known to be seventeen years old! (pp. 114–15)

I learn elsewhere that Kent County was formed in 1892, that ten years earlier only ninety-two people were in what would be the county, that Jayton, the present county seat, was founded in 1907, that Clairemont, the original county seat, consisted in 1893 of two newspapers, three saloons, and twenty people.

And elsewhere I learn that Croton Creek, which originates

northwest of Jayton, is "at times being impregnated by 450 to 660 tons of chloride escaping daily from its ancient seabed. Croton feeds this directly into the Salt Fork Brazos" (Naomi H. Kincaid, "Surface Water in West Texas," *West Texas Historical Association Year Book*, October, 1967, p. 58).

Still elsewhere, I learn that Coronado was almost certainly in southwestern Kent County in 1541, as J. W. Williams tells the story in *Old Texas Trails*.

Some come close.

The big coffee-table picture books of recent years, though, don't come close. They show no pictures of my province or even of neighboring provinces. They leave a hole in Texas that stretches southward and eastward from the Caprock down to I-20 and over to Dallas and Fort Worth. They show pictures of East Texas, of the coast, of the Hill Country (everyone has to show pictures of the Hill Country), of the Big Bend area and the Guadalupes, maybe a shot of Palo Duro Canyon. They miss the strange and lonesome beauty: the view one sees of the Double Mountains down the Salt Fork from the highway bridge between Swenson and Jayton; the first dramatic drop into the deep of the Croton Breaks just past the old Lowrance place on the edge of Jayton just past where I nearly lost a nickel; the blue wonder of Putoff Canyon just to the north of Jayton; lonesome stretches where the Caprock rears above red rough country. The picture books don't come close.

Some do, but don't quite get there. I cherish and curse Randolph Marcy and M. K. Kellogg. They were almost there, goddam them. Why in hell couldn't they get there and tell me what I've seen?

Marcy's first miss was in 1849, on his mapping expedition back from Dona Ana. His route carried him just a little to the south of the territory I wanted him to tell about, though at one time he was only about fifteen miles south of the Double Mountains (I'm judging by Grant Foreman's *Marcy and the Gold Seekers* and by J. W. Williams's "Marcy's Road from Dona Ana," *West Texas Historical Association Year Book*, October, 1943, pp. 128–52). Then in 1854, on his expedition to locate possible sites for reservations in West Texas, he came closer, though his impressions were mixed. In his letter-report to Colonel Cooper, he tells what he saw while still on the Wichita, looking across rough country toward the Brazos (he was apparently in present King County east of Dickens, toward Guthrie, but southerly):

All united in forming a landscape pleasing to the eye; but this is the only feature in the country which has left an agreeable impression upon my memory, and I bade adieu to its desolate and inhospitable borders without the least feeling of regret, for it is, in almost every repect, the most uninteresting and forbidding land I have ever visited. A barren and parsimonious soil, affording little but weeds and coarse unwholesome grass, with an intermixture of cactie of most uncomely and grotesque shapes, studded with a formidable armour of thorns which defies the approach of man or beast, added to the fact already alluded to, of the scarcity of wood or good water, would seem to render it probable that this section was not designed by the Creator for occupation, and I question if the next century will see it populated by civilized man. Even the Indians shun this country, and there were no evidences of their camps along the valley; so that the bears (which are numerous here) are left in undisturbed possession. (Foreman, p. 176)

But I owe Marcy something. He gave part of my cosmos its name. A little later, he and his group came upon a spring of fresh water. "I am not prepared to say that it was equal to Croton water cooled with Rockland ice," Marcy said, "yet I doubt if the people of Gotham ever enjoyed their boasted and justly renowned beverage more than we did." He named the small tributary into which the spring flowed "Croton Creek," whence the name "Croton Breaks." It was what we know as Little Croton; Croton and North Croton are westerly, nearer to the heart of the territory I wanted him to tell about. W. B. Parker, who accompanied Marcy on this expedition, echoes Marcy's sentiments in his *Notes Taken during the Expedition Commanded by Capt. R. B. Marcy, U.S.A., through Unexplored Texas in the Summer and Fall of 1854:*

And now having finished our perilous trip into those unexplored and inhospitable regions, and returned once more to enjoy the few comforts we left behind us, but one opinion prevailed with us, viz.: that the dangers we encountered and the privations we suffered had not been in vain, establishing as they did the fact, that for all purposes of human habitation—except it might be for a penal colony—those wilds are totally unfit. Destitute of soil, tim-

ber, water, game, and everything else that can sustain or make
life tolerable, they must remain as they are, uninhabited and un-
inhabitable.

Perhaps some use may be made of the mineral resources, but
that will have to be done under a load of peril to life, that few will
be willing to encounter, none to endure for any length of time.
Our party certainly, having left them without regret, will never return to them, except in memory, and then in reminiscences too
painful far to be pleasant. (p. 173)

M. K. Kellogg came close, but didn't leave me what I had hoped
for. An artist and world traveler, Kellogg accompanied an expedition sponsored by the Texas Land and Copper Association into
West Texas. The Association came from nowhere much and soon
disappeared, but had high hopes of finding copper lodes out toward the Double Mountains. Kellogg's notes survived in three
penciled notebooks, edited by Llerena Friend as *M. K. Kellogg's
Texas Journal 1872,* published in 1967 by the University of Texas
Press. His first entry is for May 18, 1872; his last is for September 25, 1872.

On Wednesday, July 31, he notes that the temperature is 98°
and that they are within twenty miles of Jacksboro: "I have stood
the tiresome journey very well indeed, and am cheered with the
fact that we are *now* pursuing the object of our contemplated
tour—*Double Mtns.*" For Monday, August 12, he notes the following:

> Sketched "Clear Fork" valley to S. from the E. bank of a creek empty-
> ing into the Fork from the N. The scenery is fine & soil excellent
> —with mesquite grass & a bull thistle covering the ground. In large
> masses this thistle makes a good adjunct to the foreground—like
> candelabra of many lights of brilliant purple on light pea green
> branches. The precipitous banks of these streams present strata
> horizontal of limestone blocks of good building material—and the
> ground pebbles of hard stones & flint. The swift running waters are
> musically brought to my ears by the southern breeze & grateful it
> is too—for it is the first sound of running waters which has greeted
> me on this long journey. But no cries of coyote or song of birds are
> heard.

By Thursday, August 15, the expedition is in sight of Flat Top
Mountain, and at 10:40 "descry Kiowa Peak in the distant . . .

fine range of high hills bearing N. W. 55° and the Double Mtn. also bearing S. 60 W."

> All descending from wagons & horses and group themselves together on the highest portion of our watershed and view the beautiful & long sought region with delight. The two mountains are connected by a long range of mountains of nearly equal height, very picturesque, which are called the *Mtns of the Brazos*, Double Mtn. rising above them, distinctly defined as the atmosphere intervenes.

The next morning, he notes that while he was making a pencil sketch of the Double Mountains, "the sun prostrated me so that I had to keep myself on the ground or in the ambulance—quite torpid on the brain." That day, Friday, August 16, they start for Kiowa Peak:

> We skirted the deep ravines and finally got down to its banks [the river's] over deep washings & gullies of red sand and buffalo trails —very rough—with blocks of white gypsum scattered about & other minerals & carnelians, we went into camp at 7:30 A.M. having made only 5 m. progress in 3 hours.

By mid-afternoon, they are able to overlook the "vast plains of the river ('Double Mtn Fork') to the S. W. with the whole range of Mts bounding them on the W & N":

> The view of this basin is melancholy & wild—No pastures of flowers—no large spaces covered with young green grass to cheer the spirit against the sadness produced by the knarled trunks & branches of the short & scraggy mesquite trees—without a leaf upon their dead carcasses, yet still standing & clinging to the hope of resurrection from the life yet remaining in their roots. For these are the skeletons by day & the bogies by night which spread themselves thinly over the ground in all directions. All is death, but the now parched mesquite grass which imparts health & strength to our jaded animals. Temp about 95.

But on Wednesday, August 21, Kellogg's discontent with the expedition, his complaints, and his illness have about done him in:

> Passed bad night. Quinine devils. Today fixed in ambulance—too weak to descend. Here is a party without a proper wagon for a sick man—a *rich* party sending out 50 men into an arid wilderness

without any proper means of preventive or of cure of such diseases as are known to endanger every strangers health & life. "Put not your trust in princes." I cannot return neither proceed & must endure this accursed region of 99° and no water fit to drink until such time as the Company of rich men choose—*for their own interest*, to make a way for my getting back to a civilized land. As to *Double Mts.* I can see it far off 60 m or more—that is all I wish to see of it—at present—and the Co. may yet send some of our number to explore it to save their credit—and make a "good report" to sell their bonds &c—That now is all they will or can do.

Two days later, he reports that he is "in less pain & sketched 'Double Mountains' after sunrise when its outlines were very clear. It is said to be 60 m dist."

A few days later, he was somewhat revived, as he notes for Thursday, August 29:

Determined to cross the Brazos before going back home I took a mule & accompanied by Col Johnson & Col McCarty started for Kiowa Peak at 9:00 A.M. — — cloudy rather — — and crossed the Brazos at 9 A.M.stopping to pick up precious stones on the shores —passed over in a hurry for fear of quick sand—safely—two miles below Kiowa Peak on Brazos. Now in the promised land—unlike Moses, who only *looked* across Jordan, and died—ascending breaks in the 50 [foot] high banks of the River on North side—the Southern being a low overflowing plains—of great richness.

Shortly thereafter, the expedition started back east, though a small group went on to try to reach the Double Mountains. This small group rejoins the expedition by September 4, testifying that they have climbed the Double Mountains. But when Kellogg reaches Jacksboro with the others, he meets a man named D. W. Patten, who knows the territory and who pretty well convinces Kellogg that the small group did not reach the Double Mountains, and that what Kellogg thought he was sketching was not the Double Mountains: "After a long talk with Patten I presume that Peters' party did not in fact get to the Double Mtn but only to what I drew as such which hides D. M. which lies 30 m. beyond. A *dreadful* mistake if it be one."

And there is one more mistake to record. In addition to quick little pencil sketches in his notebooks, Kellogg did water colors all along the way. At Sherman, on his way toward home, Kellogg left his sketchbook, with all his watercolors, behind. "How fearful I am that this sole evidence & labor of my long Texas trip will be lost," Kellogg writes on September 19. And it was. No one has since seen his watercolors.

Some get close, but they don't tell me what I want to hear, or show me what I want to see. All that seems to be left is my little memory text, and it fades, fades. I didn't reach the Double Mountains, either. I did not take my son to Yankee Stadium when Joe DiMaggio was hitting in 56 consecutive games. My son was born too late, and I was born too poor or too unwilling. I did not take my younger daughter down every winding country lane she wanted to see. I did not take my older daughter to Dresden, or to be Bach's pupil. I have lost the White Horse Inn and cannot find it. I did not dance her across Vienna, walk her up Vermont.

I have not seen the Altneuschul of Prague, though it has waited since the thirteenth century. Rabbi Judah Loew ben Bezalel made the Golem there. Now the synagogue serves a congregation almost gone, with no prospect of revival.

How did it look that time in Latvia when Riga fell? I'm waiting for someone to tell me. Will they ever find the treasures that one family buried deep in the yard? How shall I learn where? How it looked? By what tree?

How was it among the Comanches that morning in Palo Duro Canyon, when they looked up and saw the troopers, looked up and saw the future ending? How did Satanta and Satank and Big Tree stand upon the earth that other time, and what did they see, and why did they hurry so to die?

Perhaps if I went to San Angelo and stood on the headquarters porch at Fort Concho, perhaps I would see. Perhaps if I could get myself situated just so with the sun, I'd see how it looked to General Ranald Mackenzie. If I try again, perhaps I'll get myself situated just so with the sun.

I can't find the farmhouse. It burned some years ago, but is still plain up the rise from the highway, past the railroad trestle, alone, facing east. In bed on the screened porch, I could hear the creaking music of the porch swing, hear the creaking music of the windmill down the way, see the moon rise.

The synagogue in Budapest survived centuries, Soviets, and Nazis to house a ravaged remnant. I wander along the aisles of

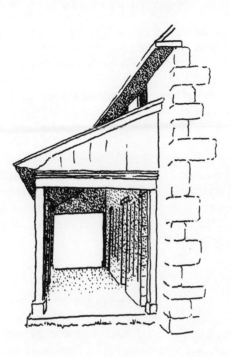

the delicatessen, reading labels, wondering how things are in
Budapest.

It's all fragmented, but only partially indexed. I can call up
pieces: a lost birthplace here, a map of the territory yonder; a mill
here, an outhouse there, ruined house and schoolteacherly aunt
over the way; a weed, a snake, a longing for food; the shadowy
indeterminacy of it all; a drought; a hope for poetry; yonder, a
little evidence that the world exists, and over there, some notion
of what changes; here a little notice of what fall will bring, there
a little account of going back. I can call up pieces, but I can't get
it all back, for I never had it all.

And all that's left now is my little memory text. It fades, fades,
and I can't get a witness.

I long for much of earth, as it is now, as it was before, as it
might be, but not for all. I have no zeal for everywhere. I can't
go everywhere, perhaps not anywhere. My time's too short. I'm

still trying to see what I see, still trying to see the places, how they looked, who was there, how things were in Budapest and Spur and down through the Croton Breaks. I've not long enough to look. I'm not quick enough to see. I'm not strong enough to search for all the rest, not brave enough to see and lose so much.

I can't catch it all, find it all, or any part wholly, or myself. All that seems to be left is my little memory text, and it fades, fades, and I can't get a witness. Does it all go, vanish from us? Do we all, in our several, small, and quirky ways, go through a holocaust or the Palo Duro Canyon, into diaspora and loneliness? If we catch energy and spirit, do we get a chance to see how things were at Grandpa's farm, to go toward Jayton, Latvia, Riga? Down through the Croton Breaks? Toward the Double Mountains? God lives on top, where I've never been.

Going Home

I wanted to go by the north route and save the south route for last, when we'd be coming home. I had no particular reason except that I know the south route better from old days. For me, it has more places, and I wanted to save it.

The route goes north of west out of Fort Worth. We went through Jacksboro, avoided the north fork to Wichita Falls, and went on through Olney and Seymour. Out of Seymour the distances grow longer, the houses are fewer, and the country is wider. Benjamin is next on this route, and then Guthrie.

When you get to Guthrie, you're in the territory. Guthrie is headquarters for the Four Sixes Ranch. On the sweeping curve just west of town, we saw again the main ranch house, just north of the highway, and the ranch commissary, just south, with four big sixes across it.

> Guthrie is the county seat of King County. The 1980–81 Texas Almanac estimates a population of 140 for the town, 400 for the county. The county covers some 944 square miles. Other towns are Dumont, Finney, and Grow, none with more than 100 souls, excluding ghosts. The county is "Hilly, broken by Wichita and Brazos tributaries; extensive grassland; dark loam to red soils." Minerals

and ranching provide most income. Average annual rainfall is under 22 inches.

I don't know King County, except the road to Dickens. The Croton Breaks stretch far into its southwestern reaches; we saw again the first ravines, red, rough, and worn, wrinkling down southward from the highway. After a while we came to what my Aunt Cora calls "Dickens Hill." It isn't a hill, I guess, but rather the last quick rise on the way up from 600 feet elevation at Fort Worth to over 2,100 at Dickens. At Dickens, we turned left, and after about five miles, we could see Soldiers Mound. That meant we were not far from Spur. Soldiers Mound, so they always told me, had its name because one of Mackenzie's cavalrymen was buried there during the campaign of 1874–75 against the Comanches. We didn't linger, though I have always wanted to know where Mackenzie camped below the Mound on Duck Creek, but went on into Spur. When I was young and sometimes went with Grandpa into town on a Saturday, Spur seemed a big town, and I thought it bustled.

However, the 1936 Texas Almanac shows a population of only 1,899. In the southern part of the county, Spur is "the principal market and shipping point." It has several cotton gins, a cotton compress, and a creamery. Dickens, the county seat of Dickens County, had a population of 256 in 1936. The county is in northwestern Texas, below the high plains, the Almanac reports and was created in 1876 and named for one J. Dickens, who died at the Alamo. The county covers some 880 square miles, with a 1936 population of about 8,600. A cotton and cattle county with a generally rolling surface, Dickens County's altitude ranges from 2,500 to 3,000 feet, and its average rainfall is 22 inches. "Loam and sandy

loam soils prevail. The county is mostly open, but has mesquite and a little cottonwood along the streams. Gypsum is found in commercial quantities."

The main street, Burlington Avenue, is dead now. Of some thirty shops opening onto the street, no more than five are in use. What I noticed first, I think, was that the Spur Cafe was closed, the place it occupied empty. Fifteen years ago, it would have been just about full every weekday morning with townfolk getting their breakfast, a few oil field workers, and ranchers and farmers in town "to do a little business." When we visited Spur once about that time, I was up early one morning. I walked a ways along Burlington Avenue and stopped in the Spur Cafe for coffee about 6:30. A copy of the morning edition of the Fort Worth *Star Telegram* was at each place down the counter. I took a stool, ordered coffee, started the paper, and then realized that I had displaced all of the regular customers by one seat each. Now the Spur Cafe is closed, the place it occupied empty. People get their breakfast and coffee at the Dairy Queen on the edge of the town. Spur bustled, I thought, when I was young. I remember when they brought the county's first bale of cotton for the year in and put it on the

sidewalk at the corner by the bank. They don't do that now, but Spur bustled, I thought when I was young. Now, most things have changed, and some things have gone.

The Almanac *for 1980–81 reports that Spur's population has dropped off to about 1,500, though Dickens is holding its own with 280. The newer account says of the physical features, "Broken land, Cap rock in northwest; sandy, chocolate, red soils; drains to Croton, Duck Creeks." Croton Creek rises along in the middle of the county and twists southeastward through the Croton Breaks, which fill the southeastern quadrant. Recreation is "hunting, fishing, local events," and there is a small oil and gas output. Average rainfall has dropped to about 20 inches.*

Spur seemed to bustle when I was young, but little is left that I remember. Places stand empty, and the people I knew are dead or gone.

At the cemetery just outside of town, we found the graves of Ernest and Pearl Durham, my mother's parents, my Grandpa and Grandma. They lie on the high eastern edge of the slope. The message carved across the common stone reads, "They may rest from their labors." We came upon graves marked with simple wooden crosses, mostly rotting. A good many graves made in the

1920s and 1930s are marked with rough concrete slabs, some decorated with broken pieces of colored glass. One William L. Smith,
born January 23, 1938, died July 29, 1938, was commemorated with
a rough concrete marker in which his name had been spelled out
with bright marbles. High on the back side of the cemetery, we
found a state memorial marker, "In memory of Privates Gregg,
William Max, W. H. Kilpatrick and Other Soldiers Who met death
in this region while serving under General R. S. Mackenzie,
Fourth U.S. Cavalry 1871–2 and 1874–5. With no hope of honor
if victorious, no dream of mercy if they fell, and the certainty
of death by torture if taken alive, they fought the savage Comanche and cleared the plains for the White men."

We looked awhile through Spur and turned away, southeast-
erly now along State Highway 70 toward Gilpin, Girard, and
Jayton, down in Kent County. Gilpin, though it still shows on
the map, was never more than a filling station with some groceries
and a post office, and next door a small house where the owner-
postmaster lived. One summer, long ago, when I had spent a week
or so with my Grandpa and Grandma, they arranged for me to
go home by train from Gilpin to Jayton, some twenty-five miles.
The postmaster put out a flag so the train that came up from
Stamford through Jayton to Spur every morning and back in the
afternoon would stop for me. My Grandma outfitted me for the
trip with a sack of tea cakes, and it was the grandest experience
I had known, sitting in the caboose, where there were (I think)
four fine two-person seats, and the smell of leather and polished
wood was maybe the richest smell I'd known.

The train stopped running long ago, Gilpin is empty, and no

flag flies. They've taken up the tracks, and the high trestle where I used to play below my Grandpa's house is gone. The house is gone, too. It burned, they tell me, a few years back, but it was long since vacant.

I remember a time when my family drove up from Jayton to see Grandma and Grandpa. The road took us into the northwest, and we faced a scary dark line storm. It raged on by us, though, whipping us a little with its tail, and we got some hard rain and a little hail. By the time we got there, it had passed and the sun was out. When we pulled up to the house and parked by the kerosene barrel that I rode for a horse, we could see Grandpa's crop lying beaten flat in the field, ruined by the heavy hail that caught them. By the time we got out of the car, the two of them were standing at the door waiting for us. Grandma had flour on her face and down her front. "Pa came to the house," she said, "and said there wasn't anything to do out there, so I thought I'd just make some tea cakes."

I remember, too, the long table where we ate (children last if there were many), and the rough bench against the wall behind it. My Aunt Cora tells me that when I was very young I hid empty corn cobs under the bench so no one would know how many I'd had, but later, when I spent time there in the summer, there was no need to hide them—Grandma would keep providing ears of corn as long as I would eat.

And I remember the screened porch across the east of the house. At the south end there was a wooden swing that would hold three if they crowded. At the north end was a bed, where I slept on summer visits. Nights might have ruined alimentary systems. Once it was dark, the outhouse was out of the question. It was spidery in sunlight; in the dark, no right-thinking person would go there. The best one could manage was to run hurriedly into the dark at the edge of the yard and pee hard in wide circles to discourage the snakes that might be waiting.

I remember my Grandpa in the field, plowing, and at the barn in his continuing debates with the big plow horse, Prince. I remember my Grandma with flour on her face and generally smelling sweet and powdery. But mostly I remember the porch at night. When the moon was full, it came up right over the trestle, and the swing at the other end of the porch would sing a little as it moved in the night breeze, and I could hear the creaking turn of the windmill down the way. The windmill and the barn are still standing, but everything else is gone from that slope I remember.

From Gilpin we tried out a dirt road to the east, thinking to find a way into the Croton Breaks. Before long, all promising turns were either too chancy or posted or both, and we turned back. Another dirt road out from Gilpin went by where the Duck Creek School used to be, and I could see where the Big Rock Candy Mountain was before they chewed it all up into gravel to make Highway 70. After a while, we turned back out onto the highway, backtracked toward Spur, and took the two-lane highway to Clairemont. I don't think I ever traveled that stretch before, but once we got to Clairemont and headed on toward Rotan, I remember a little about the country, chiefly that the road would take us around the north end of the Double Mountains along a rough-etched piece of country. I remember coming once or twice from Jayton through Clairemont to Rotan, but Rotan was the end of the world in that direction for me.

So again it was new country that we drove through from Rotan to Aspermont, and I saw for the first time the back side of the Double Mountains. Sometimes, even now, it seems that I've always been looking at the Double Mountains, but I'd never seen their back side. I expect that people who live on what I call their back side think they live on the front side, and if asked would reckon that all this time I've been looking at them hind-side-to. Maybe so. I don't think so.

We stopped in Aspermont and took a room at Hickman's Motel and Restaurant, Phone 817-989-3531, Hi-way 380 and 83, Aspermont, Texas, 79502, where we stayed for the rest of our grand tour. Our neighbors in the motel were mostly oil crews. Aspermont is the county seat of Stonewall County. I was born in Stonewall County, in the country much closer to Jayton over in Kent County than to Aspermont. I had never stopped before to think about the name of the town. It isn't on a mountain, but the stars are close and bright.

Stonewall County, the 1980–81 Almanac *says, is northwest, below the Caprock. It covers 926 square miles, and 1,430 voters are*

*registered. "Oil, agribusiness leading economic factors." Asper-
mont, the county seat, has a population of 1,169, and is the center
for oil field and ranching operations. The county is level, bisected
by the Brazos forks, with "sandy loam, sandy; other soils; some
hills." The Double Mountain Fork of the Brazos twists all over the
north half of the county. In the northwest corner of the county,
Croton Creek and Salt Croton join the Salt Fork.*

On the first day, we didn't do much. Early, we drove north
toward Guthrie, up along the eastern rim of the Croton Breaks.
Once or twice we tried dirt roads westward, to see what we could
see of the rough beginnings of the Breaks, but after a while we
drove back to Aspermont, stopping only to watch two sleek small
planes spraying some wild country, perhaps to kill the mesquite
ahead of cultivation. Out of Aspermont this time we drove to-

ward the Double Mountains. We had no route, but took the likeliest-looking dirt ruts toward the mountains.

When I was young and my family lived in Jayton, I could see the Double Mountains almost anytime I chose. They were always blue in the distance, as they are now in my memory, and I long ago concluded that God lives up on top. Even when we topped the mesa just outside Aspermont, they were still blue, though near. Our errant course took us closer and closer—we stopped once to look through the Double Mountain Cemetery— and eventually, as we came upon them the colors came through the blue, and we could see them right before us. But we never actually reached the Double Mountains. By and by, we came to a last ravine, a fence, and a gate marked POSTED, and could go no farther. We went back to Aspermont, to try other routes the next day after we had breakfast with oil crews and others native to the Hickman Restaurant.

This time, at last, we headed toward Jayton. We had just about circled the place in days before, but I was waiting to look more carefully there, and I still wasn't ready.

We left Aspermont, rounded the mesa outside town, and the Double Mountains were there again on our left to the south. We went through Swenson. There was never much there, and there's less now. Not far from Swenson we came to the Salt Fork of the Brazos. The view of the Double Mountains down the mostly dry riverbed is still, to my mind, the perfect image. Once my father's family and some of my mother's family were strewn all over the west bank of the Salt Fork. Uncle Jack's farm was there, and Uncle Alec's. The farms are still there, but other folks own them. Just beyond them was the Reece place, where my mother's parents first sharecropped when they came to West Texas in 1919 after the boll weevils had taken Grandpa's crop near Denton. The remnant of the house still stands, long unused. The porch has fallen off, and the windows are gone, and the weeds grow into the house. Nearby is the rise where the Center View Church and the Center View School once stood. They're long gone, but I remember my mother and father talking of being students at the school together. We went through Jayton, and I tried not to look much this time.

Northwest of Jayton, back on Highway 70 toward Spur, we took

a dirt road into the Croton Breaks. It twisted generally eastward, narrowing and growing rougher as we went. At one point, the road took us to just about one farm's length of the Salt Flats on Salt Croton Creek. Buffalo hunters gathered there in the 1870s and 1880s to treat the meat and hides they'd won from the slaughter. My father remembers going with his father by wagon to the Flats to get salt. Swimming was good there, he says, and the salt was clean enough to use on the table, though most used it for curing meat and for salt licks. The way into the Salt Flats is posted, too. I understand about posting, I guess, to keep strangers out, and dumb hunters who might shoot a cow for a deer. I know about privacy and might put POSTED signs up myself if I lived behind some gates. Still, I wished they'd let me in. We drove on. Farther down the narrowing road we came to Croton Creek and crossed it on the plank bridge, each plank lifting and slapping as we passed.

After a while, we came back out onto the highway near Swenson and returned to Jayton, but I still didn't look. Instead, we went to the cemetery just north of town. It is still what I thought it was then, those years ago, the lonesomest place on earth. It's still surrounded by the fields that reach up to the edge of town. If you stand there and look west, you can see forever. There are names there I know, all over—my brother's best friend, a man I knew as a boy when we were in the same class for the better part of four years (he died in Korea, and I didn't), and others. On the western edge, in maybe the lonesomest place, my father's mother and father lie. I didn't know them in the same way that I knew my other grandparents. My father's father died when I was eight and not yet thinking much. My father's mother lived on for a good many years, always lost without her husband, but she was a stranger to me, and that's another story. We came away then and went back to the Hickman Motel and Restaurant. That was enough for the day. I had saved a day to walk and drive in Jayton itself.

Jayton is in Kent County, formed in 1876, organized in 1892, named for Andrew Kent, who died at the Alamo. The area is 875 square miles. The Almanac *for 1936 reports a population of 3,851. In 1936, 33,697 acres were harvested out of a total tilled and raw land available of 70,338 acres. "Located a short distance below the cap rock escarpment, Kent County has a level to rolling surface, with some hills. Altitude, 2000 to 2800 feet. Rainfall, about 22.72 inches. The soils are mainly loam and sandy loam. Much of the county is wooded with mesquite." In 1936, Clairemont, population 210, was the county seat. Jayton, population 623 in 1936, "is a railroad shipping point. It has a cottonseed oilmill."*

We went back to Jayton early the next morning and parked by the new courthouse in the square. Now Jayton is the county seat. When we lived there, the square was empty, and town was arranged around it, though for a while there was a place there with only posts for walls where folks danced. I remember hearing the grown people being scandalized one Sunday morning at church—word had already gotten around town that they had danced there Saturday night to "When the Saints Go Marching In," and I guess that was the most sinful thing I'd heard about then since the time I vaguely came to understand that Uncle Carl drank a bit. Three of the four sides of the square were mostly strange to me, and the fourth was a ruin. On the east side, Mr. Robinson's grocery store was gone. There never was much on the south side except the Ford place and a little brick shop that housed the Public Utilities Commission. They were still there, though changed. The north side was entirely new to me. Bryant-Links Dry Goods Store was gone, and so was Jones's Drug Store. At the northwest corner the other grocery store was gone, and the Texas Theater next to it was gone (when I was young, it was sometimes open), and beyond it Huls Drug Store was gone and the doctor's office above it. Only one small house stood in their place. The old bank on the west side and the ugly post office behind it were still there, but crumbling. Beside the new bank along the west side of the square there still stood two buildings that I knew, the Barfoot Hotel—a two-story marvel that was vaguely Spanish and had maybe twelve or fifteen rooms—and the little building with the big glass windows that once housed the Jayton *Chronicle*, the weekly newspaper. I really don't remember quite why or how, but I spent some time there when I was young. I peered inside and saw that old tires and parts of cars were scattered about the place.

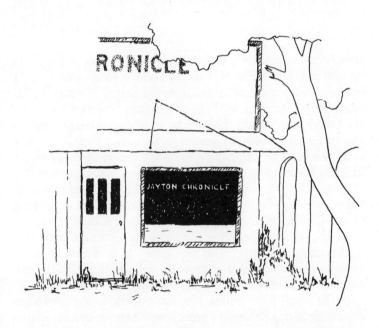

After that, we drove and walked around the town. I remembered many of the houses we saw, but many that I remembered were gone. The first house my family lived in when we came to Jayton was gone. (My memory of the time before holds only a quick image or two.) The second house we lived in was gone. The

third house we lived in was gone. My family, you see, knew about upward mobility before the phrase became popular. We slowly moved upward, there in Jayton, from ramshackle poverty to nice poor. The fourth house we lived in was gone. The fifth house—in the Lowrance place on the far edge of town, where the first ravine of the Croton Breaks was at our back door—was being used as a hay barn. The sixth house was still there, and in good repair. The last house we lived in before we moved to the city was still there, and looked better than when we left all those years ago. Someone did several good paint jobs and covered the sides with stucco. The fence where I lost a nickel was still there, up across a corner of the field from the Lowrance place, but the fence that my brother didn't quite jump was gone. My best friend's house was gone; my next-best friend's house was still there. The school I went to had been taken down, and a handsome new school had taken its place. It seemed well appointed; the football field has grass, lights, and a closed-in press box. When my brother played football at Jayton, I remember watching the principal draw off the yard markers in the dirt with a hoe. The town is mostly poor, and the people are mostly old, but the school has prospered as a consequence of oil money and consolidation of all the county schools in the one place. Since we were at the school building, we drove and measured the distance to the Lowrance place, the longest walk I had. It was barely a mile, though I've no doubt told my children it was upwards of three.

According to the new Almanac, *Jayton held its own, with a population of 686 in 1980 as compared with 623 in 1936. Kent County's appearance is now described as "rolling, broken terrain; drains to Salt and Double Mountain Forks, Brazos River; sandy, loam soils." Recreation includes "hunting, local events; scenic croton breaks and salt flat." The county's business is agribusiness and oil field operations, and Jayton, the county seat, is described as a "farm trade center."*

Finally, we drove just past the Lowrance place again—the Lowrances are long dead—to the spot where Putoff Canyon begins right at the side of Highway 70 northwest of Jayton. The canyon goes deep rapidly though it's narrow at the bottom, and if you sit at the little rest stop by the side of the road, you can see a long way into Croton Breaks, and the rough country lies blue in the distance. I don't know how far I ever walked into the Breaks when I was young, not too far, I'd guess, but I always thought there was magic deep in there some place. I thought then and I think now that if I would just look hard enough I would find it.

After a while we drove away, back to Aspermont, and joined the oil crews for dinner at the Hickman Restaurant.

The next morning we left early for home, taking the south route we had saved for last. Out of Aspermont we passed Old Glory and Sagerton and stopped to read the marker just outside Stamford that mapped out Mackenzie's trail to the Comanches in Palo Duro Canyon. From Stamford we went through Avoca and Leuders to Albany, just south of old Fort Griffin, where the buffalo hunters gathered going and coming on the great hunts that ended the herds.

The herds are gone. The trestle is gone. My grandparents are gone. Their houses are gone. Bryant-Links Dry Goods Store is gone, and the grocery store, and Huls Drug Store, and the Texas Theater. The Croton Breaks are well fenced and posted, and I expect it's only possible to know them afoot. The Jayton *Chronicle* office looks like an old garage, and the Barfoot Hotel was abandoned long ago. Things change. We change. Perhaps the past is always being lopped off behind us; when all the past has been lopped off, we will die, or be otherwise.

From Albany we drove on to Breckenridge, then through the pleasant rough country on either side of the Brazos and through Palo Pinto to Mineral Wells, Weatherford, and then we were home.

At dinner that evening, I was trying to tell our daughter about the changes, the empty farmhouses gone to agribusiness, the places gone or abandoned. I told her about the Texas Theater and the trestle and Grandpa's house.

"Daddy," she asked, "what did you expect?"

I don't know. Once my people and houses I knew were scattered all over the territory. Now they are gone. The wind passes over the places where they were, and they are gone, and the places where they were will know them no more. We won't go back much any more.

What did I expect? Nothing much, daughter my love, nothing much. Perhaps a trace or two of myself. Perhaps some clue to tell why I still think God lives on top of the Double Mountains, and a ravine and a fence and a posted sign still stand in my way. Little more. It was never Eden.